Zero-Base Budgeting

WILEY SERIES ON SYSTEMS AND CONTROLS FOR FINANCIAL MANAGEMENT

Edited by Robert L. Shultis and Frank M. Mastromano

EDP Systems for Credit Management
Conon D. Whiteside

Profile for Profitability
Thomas S. Dudick

Zero-Base Budgeting
Peter A. Pyhrr

Zero-Base Budgeting

A PRACTICAL MANAGEMENT TOOL FOR EVALUATING EXPENSES

PETER A. PYHRR

Vice President Finance
Alpha Wire Corp.
Elizabeth, New Jersey

Professional Associate
Management Analysis Center, Inc. (Management Consultants)
Cambridge (Mass.) · Northbrook (Chicago) · Washington · Palo Alto

A Wiley-Interscience Publication

JOHN WILEY & SONS   New York • London • Sydney • Toronto

Library of Congress Cataloging in Publication Data:

Pyhrr, Peter A   1942-
    Zero-base budgeting.

    (Wiley series on systems and controls for
financial management)
    "A Wiley-Interscience publication."
    1. Budget in business. 2. Budget.
3. Program budgeting. I. Title.

HF5550.P95   658.1′54   72-8358
ISBN 0-471-70234-X

Printed in the United States of America

10

To C. J. "Tommy" Thomsen, member of the Board of Directors, Cecil Dotson, Grant Dove, Jim Fischer, and Bryan Smith, Vice-Presidents, of Texas Instruments, who saw the need for and were the first to adopt the zero-base budgeting process; and to Governor Jimmy Carter of Georgia, whose desire to improve the effectiveness and efficiency of State Government led to the adoption of the process in Georgia; plus Tish and Eric.

SERIES PREFACE

No one needs to tell the reader that the world is changing. He sees it all too clearly. The immutable, the constant, the unchanging of a decade or two ago no longer represent the latest thinking—on *any* subject, whether morals, medicine, politics, economics, or religion. Change has always been with us, but the pace has been accelerating, especially in the postwar years.

Business, particularly with the advent of the electronic computer some 20 years ago, has also undergone change. New disciplines have sprung up. New professions are born. New skills are in demand. And the need is ever greater to blend the new skills with those of the older professions to meet the demands of modern business.

The accounting and financial functions certainly are no exception. The constancy of change is as pervasive in these fields as it is in any other. Industry is moving toward an integration of many of the information gathering, processing, and analyzing functions under the impetus of the so-called systems approach. Such corporate territory has been, traditionally, the responsibility of the accountant and the financial man. It still is, to a large extent—but times are changing.

Does this, then, spell the early demise of the accountant as we know him today. Does it augur a lessening of influence for the financial specialists in today's corporate hierarchy? We think not. We maintain, however, that it is incumbent upon today's accountant and today's financial man to learn *today's* thinking and to *use today's* skills. It is for this reason the Wiley Series on Systems and Controls for Financial Management is being developed.

Recognizing the broad spectrum of interests and activities that the series title encompasses, we plan a number of volumes, each representing the latest thinking, written by a recognized authority, on a particular facet of the financial man's responsibilities. The subjects contemplated for discussion within the series range from production accounting systems to planning, to corporate records, to control of cash. Each book is an in-depth study of one subject within this group. Each is intended to be a practical, working tool for the businessman in general and the financial man and accountant in particular.

ROBERT L. SHULTIS

FRANK M. MASTROMANO

WHY ZERO-BASE BUDGETING?

The need for an effective budget procedure is increasingly apparent in both industry and government today. All institutions must adapt to an environment in which the allocation of resources presents a constantly deepening challenge, with corporations facing decreasing profits, spiraling costs, and increasing pressures to hold down prices, and with governments going bankrupt in the face of ever increasing demands and costs for services. To effectively allocate limited resources, a budget procedure must determine simultaneously the answer to two questions:

1. Where and how can we most effectively spend our money?
2. How much money should we spend? (What should the dollar amount of limited resources be? We can always increase expenditures in industry at the expense of profits or increase expenditures in government at the expense of the taxpayer!)

To answer these questions, most corporations and government agencies use the current operating and expenditure levels as an established base, from which they analyze in detail only those increases (or decreases) desired—thus looking at only a small fraction of the final budget dollars approved. This typical approach leaves two significant questions unanswered:

- How efficient and effective are the current operations that were not evaluated?
- Should current operations be reduced in order to fund higher priority new programs or increase profits?

I first became involved in budgeting in 1968 in the Staff and Research divisions of Texas Instruments. At this time we were facing a budget decrease. If we were looking for a 5% decrease, we asked managers to identify what they would reduce if their budgets were cut 10%—and then we chose the 5% reduction from the 10% identified. After the budgets were set, a senior vice-president by the name of Cecil Dotson said, "I know in detail what you're *not* going to do, I would now like to find out what you *are* going to do," and then proceeded to hold a series of meetings to review the programs of each department. During this review, three problems were identified that I think are common in budget procedures throughout industry and government:

1. Some goals and objectives had not been established, or stated goals and objectives as understood and anticipated by top management were not realistic in light of the final amount of money budgeted. (In my conversations with several other companies, I have been told that they first establish their budgets and then determine their goals and objectives —which seems to put the cart before the horse.)

2. Some operating decisions had not been made that affected the amount of money required. I remember that we had identified a shortage of electrical capacity for the Dallas, Texas, manufacturing needs for the coming year, but we had not determined which of three possible alternatives to select to solve this problem. We had identified alternatives to (1) purchase the additional capacity from the power company, which would cost a premium since the capacity was needed at a peak load period when the rates were highest; (2) purchase additional capital equipment; or (3) transfer some temporarily excess and backup equipment from our Attleboro, Massachusetts, location to cover our needs. Each of these alternatives had significantly different budget and cash flow impacts, but this consideration fell into the crack as far as the budget development was concerned.

3. Budget dollars were not strictly allocated in accordance with changing responsibilities and work loads. Some work loads had increased significantly while others had decreased, yet everyone had his budget cut from 1 to 10%. This mismatch between the job to be done and the budget allocation was identified and corrected only because we went through this detailed analysis after the budgets were set.

At the end of this review we concluded that we wanted some type of budgeting procedure that would force us to identify and analyze what we were going to do in total, set goals and objectives, make the necessary operating decisions, and evaluate changing responsibilities and work loads—not after the budgeting process, but during it, as an integral part of the process.

From the identification of these desires, I developed the planning and budgeting methodology that we termed zero-base budgeting. (The basic concept of attempting to reevaluate all programs and expenditures every year—hence the term zero-base—is not new. However, to my knowledge the only formalized attempt at zero-base budgeting was an unsuccessful attempt by the Department of Agriculture in the early 1960's, which did not resemble the methodology used successfully in both industry and government as described in this book, although some recent developments in budget procedures are headed in the direction of zero-base budgeting.) This process was used to prepare the 1970 budget for the Staff and Research divisions of Texas Instruments. The implementation of zero-base budgeting was a team effort across all Staff and Research departments, headed by a member of the Board of Directors, C. J. (Tommy) Thomsen, and vice-presidents Cecil Dotson, Grant Dove, Jim Fischer, and Bryan Smith. Zero-base budgeting was then expanded throughout all divisions of Texas Instruments to prepare the 1971 budget.

After the implementation of zero-base budgeting in Texas Instruments, I wrote an article describing the process for the November/December 1970 issue of the *Harvard Business Review*. This article was subsequently read by the then newly elected Governor of Georgia, Jimmy Carter, who thought that the process was needed and could be effectively applied to the State of Georgia. I subsequently left Texas Instruments to help install zero-base budgeting for Governor Carter, and it was used to develop the entire executive budget recommendation for the State of Georgia for Fiscal Year 1973 (July 1972–June 1973). Since then, the process has been adopted by other corporations and governmental agencies.

The philosophy and procedures used to install zero-base budgeting in industry and government (as well as the benefits obtained and the general problems faced) are almost identical, with the mechanics differing slightly in each case to fit the needs of each user. The process requires each manager to justify his entire budget request in detail, and puts the burden of proof on him to justify why he should spend any money. Each manager must prepare a "decision package" for each activity or operation, and this package includes an analysis of cost, purpose, alternative courses of action, measures of performance, consequences of not performing the activity, and benefits. The analysis of alternatives as required by zero-base budgeting introduces a new concept to typical budgeting techniques. Managers must first identify different ways of performing each activity—such as centralizing versus decentralizing operations, or evaluating the economy of in-house print shops versus commercial printers. In addition, zero-base budgeting requires that managers identify different levels of effort for performing each activity. They must identify a minimum level of spending—often about 75% of their current operating level—and then identify in separate decision packages the costs and benefits of additional levels of spending for that activity. This analysis forces every manager to consider and evaluate a level of spending lower than his current operating level; gives management the alternative of eliminating an activity or choosing from several levels of effort; and allows tremendous trade-offs and shifts in expenditure levels among organizational units.

Once the decision packages have been developed, they must be ranked or listed in order of importance. This ranking process allows each manager to explicitly identify his priorities, merges decision packages for ongoing and new programs into one ranking, and allows top management to evaluate and compare the relative needs and priorities of different organizations to make funding decisions. As the list of decision packages increases the cost also increases, and top management can decide at what point on the list the added costs outweigh the benefits. Decision packages of lower priority—below that point—would not be funded.

Zero-base budgeting provides top management with detailed information concerning the money needed to accomplish desired ends. It spotlights redundancies and duplication of efforts among departments, focuses on dollars needed for programs rather than on the percentage increase (or decrease) from the previous year, specifies priorities within and among departments and divisions, allows comparisons across these organizational lines as to the respective priorities funded, and allows a performance audit to determine whether each activity or operation performed as promised. Changes in desired expenditure levels do not require the recycling of budget inputs, but the decision package ranking identifies those activities and operations (decision packages) to be added or deleted to produce the budget change. The list of ranked packages can also be used during the operating year to identify activities to be reduced or expanded if allowable expenditure levels change or actual costs vary from the budget. The process also gives top management a good tool with which to judge the performance of employees, and through the necessary involvement of managers at all organizational levels it gives managers a greater sense of responsibility for their budgets and the tasks they have committed to in order to obtain their budgets.

In the long run, the most significant impact from zero-base budgeting will occur in the middle and lower levels of management, where managers will have to evaluate in detail their planning, operations, efficiency, and cost effectiveness on a continuous basis. In industry, corporate profits should be improved because high priority new programs will be funded in part by improved efficiency and elimination or reduction of those current activities ·of lesser importance to the organization. In government, the taxpayer should benefit because high priority new programs can be funded at the expense of obsolete or redundant programs without significant reductions in service.

PETER A. PYHRR

Wheeling, Illinois
May 1972

CONTENTS

Zero-Base Budgeting

CHAPTER 1

THE ZERO-BASE BUDGETING PROCESS

On December 2, 1969 at the Plaza Hotel in New York City, Dr. Arthur F. Burns, then counselor to the President of the United States, addressed the annual dinner meeting of the Tax Foundation on the "Control of Government Expenditures." In this speech Dr. Burns identified the basic need for zero-base budgeting, but he also expressed his concern that such a process would be difficult if not impossible to implement:

> Customarily, the officials in charge of an established program have to justify only the increase which they seek above last year's appropriation. In other words, what they are already spending is usually accepted as necessary, without examination. Substantial savings could undoubtedly be realized if [it were required that] every agency . . . make a case for its entire appropriation request each year, just as if its program or programs were entirely new. Such budgeting procedure may be difficult to achieve, partly because it will add heavily to the burdens of budget-making, and partly also because it will be resisted by those who fear that their pet programs would be jeopardized by a system that subjects every . . . activity to annual scrutiny of its costs and results.

However, as experience in Texas Instruments, Inc. and the State of Georgia has indicated, this kind of budgeting need not "add heavily to the burdens of budget-making." In fact, effectively planned and properly managed, zero-base budgeting can actually reduce the burdens of budget making while significantly improving management decision making and the allocation of resources.

The zero-base budgeting process, as used by both Texas Instruments and the State of Georgia, is identical in philosophy and general procedures, although the specific mechanics of implementation differ slightly

1

to fit the particular needs of each organization. Zero-base budgeting is readily adaptable to organizations that have significantly different operations, needs, and problems, and the following chapters will discuss the available adaptations that make this budgeting process an effective management tool in both industry and government.

THE PLANNING AND BUDGETING PROCESSES IN PERSPECTIVE

Many managers have suggested that zero-base budgeting be renamed "zero-base planning" or "zero-base planning and budgeting" because the process requires effective planning and immediately shows up any lack of planning. The planning and budgeting process can be contrasted as follows:

Planning   identifies the *output* desired.
Budgeting identifies the *input* required.

Planning is more general than budgeting. Planning establishes programs, sets goals and objectives, and makes basic policy decisions for the organization as a whole. Budgeting analyzes in detail the many functions or activities that the organization must perform to implement each program, analyzes the alternatives within each activity to achieve the end product desired, and identifies the trade-offs between partial or complete achievement of the established goals and the associated costs. Exhibit 1-1 shows the relationship required between planning and budgeting. This relationship is dynamic because the resources required to achieve the desired goals are not unlimited. Therefore, we must determine whether achieving the last 10% of each goal requires 25% of the cost, or vice versa; whether we *can* achieve each goal; and whether we must eliminate and/or reduce some goals. If we fixed our goals, the zero-base budgeting process would be a suboptimization tool, telling us how best to achieve the given results. However, the realistic requirement to modify goals based on a cost/benefit analysis makes the zero-base budgeting process both a suboptimization and total-optimization tool.

If we take a look at this same budgeting and planning relationship from the point of view of those managers who will design and implement programs and activities to achieve the desired goals, we have the relationship shown in Exhibit 1-2. These managers need to have an understanding of the current organization and operations before they can design each program. This need is created by several factors:

Exhibit 1-1

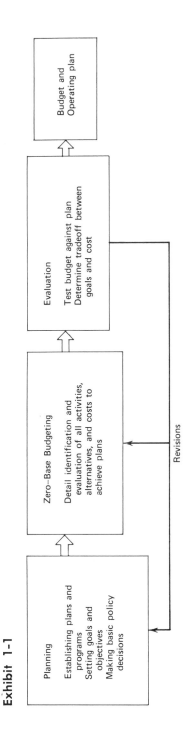

Planning

Establishing plans and programs
Setting goals and objectives
Making basic policy decisions

Zero–Base Budgeting

Detail identification and evaluation of all activities, alternatives, and costs to achieve plans

Evaluation

Test budget against plan
Determine tradeoff between goals and cost

Budget and Operating plan

Revisions

Exhibit 1-2

Basis (Starting Point)	Direction (How To Get There)	Goals (Ending Point)
A. Ideal planning situation Detailed knowledge of current activities and operations, including costs and efficiency	Detailed evaluation of directions, activities, and programs, with specific expenditures and set of established priorities with each program	Realistic, measurable, and attainable goals; with established expenditure ranges, and a set of priorities among goals
B. Poor planning situation Lack of detailed understanding of activities, costs, and efficiency	Programs and directions very broad and general; no cost guidelines; operating managers have few or no specific directions	"Motherhood" statements (increase profits; provide the best education possible; reduce air pollution; etc.)
C. Impact of zero-base budgeting Current activities, alternatives, costs, benefits, and effectiveness evaluated in detail	Identifies and evaluates both current and new activities and programs in detail: alternatives, costs, benefits, and effectiveness; establishes priorities within each program, identifying level of goal achievement at varying expenditure levels	Identifies trade-offs among programs and goals so that top management can make the decision as to what funding level they can afford versus the programs and goals they must afford to do without

Modification

Modification

4

- Goals may be achieved through extensions of current programs.
- New programs must still operate within the total organizational framework and may require support from existing activities.
- Costs may depend heavily on the effectiveness and efficiency of current activities or may reflect the capability of the organization to develop effective and efficient activities for new programs.
- Cost constraints may require the funding of new high priority programs and goals at the expense of current programs and lower priority goals.

From this basis (or starting point) managers can build programs, either modifying them to fit the capabilities of the current operations or designing them to change the current operations and modifying the goals to meet the capabilities of the programs, and then modifying both goals and programs to meet cost limitations. This determination is an interactive process that can be achieved by effective preliminary planning and the zero-base budgeting process.

Regardless of the budgeting technique used, there is no substitute for good planning. If we should not have been producing the product or providing the service in the first place, even the best operating plan and detailed budget will not buy us anything. At the very least, any budgeting system should point out such a mistake, but a lot of time and money can be saved if this conclusion is reached in the preliminary planning stage.

THE TWO BASIC STEPS OF ZERO-BASE BUDGETING

There are two basic steps of zero-base budgeting:

1. *Developing "decision packages."* This step involves analyzing and describing each discrete activity—current as well as new, in one or more decision packages. (These packages are discussed below.)

2. *Ranking "decision packages."* This step involves evaluating and ranking these packages in order of importance through cost/benefit analysis or subjective evaluation.

Once decision packages are developed and ranked, management can allocate resources accordingly—funding the most important activities (or decision packages), whether they are current or new. The final budget is produced by taking packages that are approved for funding, sorting them into their appropriate budget units, and adding up the costs identified on each package to produce the budget for each unit.

Step 1: Developing Decision Packages

Concept of Decision Packages. A decision package is a document that identifies and describes a specific activity in such a manner that management can (1) evaluate it and rank it against other activities competing for limited resources, and (2) decide whether to approve or disapprove it. Therefore, the information displayed on each package must provide management with all needed information for such evaluation. We can generally define the decision package as follows:

A decision package identifies a discrete activity, function, or operation in a definitive manner for management evaluation and comparison with other activities. This identification includes:

- Purpose (or goals and objectives)
- Consequences of not performing the activity
- Measures of performance
- Alternative courses of action
- Costs and benefits

The activities for which decision packages should be prepared—including all information required for management evaluation—will vary slightly among different organizations and will be discussed in detail in Chapters 3 and 4.

The key to zero-base budgeting lies in the identification and evaluation of alternatives for each activity. Two types of alternatives should be considered when developing decision packages:

1. *Different ways of performing the same function.* This analysis identifies alternative ways of performing a function. The best alternative is chosen and the others are discarded.

- If an alternative to the current way of doing business is chosen, the recommended way should be shown in the decision package and the current way should be shown as an alternative.
- Only one decision package is prepared. It shows the recommended way of performing the function and identifies the alternative ways considered, giving a brief explanation of why they were not chosen.

2. *Different levels of effort of performing the function.* This analysis identifies alternative levels of effort and spending to perform a specific

function. A minimum level of effort should be established, and additional levels of effort identified as separate decision packages.

• This minimum level of effort package may not completely achieve the purpose of the function (even the additional levels of effort proposed may not completely achieve it, because of realistic budget and achievement levels), but it should identify and attack the most important elements.
• In many cases, the minimum level of effort will be between 50–70% of the current level of operation. (One exception to this rule of thumb would be start-up functions or operations that were not up to full speed during the preceding budget year.)
• The minimum level of effort package would be ranked higher than the additional level(s) of effort so that the elimination of these lower ranked packages does not preclude the performance of higher ranked packages.

Managers should consider both types of alternatives in identifying and evaluating each function. Managers will usually identify different ways of performing the same function first, and then evaluate different levels of effort for performing the function for whatever way or method chosen.

The most common questions asked at this point are:

• Why should different levels of effort be identified?
• Why should a manager not choose the level of effort he thinks necessary, and then recommend that level?

Perhaps the most significant result of zero-base budgeting comes from identifying and evaluating different levels of effort. There are two reasons for this:

1. Limited expenditure levels (owing to dollar constraints and the desired funding of new or expanding programs) would cause the complete elimination of some functions if only one decision package at some desired level of effort were identified. Such elimination *might not* be desirable and practical, and higher management usually prefers to have the option of reducing current levels of effort in addition to eliminating entire functions.

2. The functional level managers who develop these decision packages are the ones who are best equipped (because of their detailed knowledge

of their particular function) to identify and evaluate different levels of effort, and it should be the responsibility of these managers to advise higher management of all possibilities. It then becomes higher management's responsibility to evaluate the relative importance of functions and the different levels of effort within each function.

Example of Production Planning. The following example of production planning illustrates the type of analysis that each manager needs to make to prepare his decision packages.

The production planning manager analyzed his department's purpose and efforts and decided that decision packages should be developed around production planning as a whole, rather than around separate work units within the department (such as working with marketing to determine delivery schedules, estimating production time and material needs, preparing schedules, etc.), since he had a small department and each work unit took only a fraction of the daily effort. He then proceeded to make the following analysis:

1. *Different ways of performing the same function.*
(a) *Recommended decision package.* Production planning department for product X, with five production planners (cost—$60,000). Maintain current organization and method of operation. This level of effort is required to maintain shipping and production schedules and inventory reports updated at the level desired by the manufacturing superintendent.
(b) *Alternatives not recommended.*

• Eliminate production planners and let line foremen do their own planning (zero incremental cost for foreman). This would result in excessive inventories, inefficient production runs, and delayed shipments.
• Combine production planning for products X, Y, and Z. This would save two planners at $15,000 each (total of 12 planners for combined departments), but foremen of each product line fear lack of specialized service; peak work loads on all product lines coincide, creating excessive burden for one supervisor; product departments are in separate buildings and physical proximity of planning is desired.

Once he had defined the basic alternatives and chosen the one he considered best, this manager completed his analyses by identifying and analyzing the different levels of effort for his chosen alternative. In this particular case he believed he could eliminate one planner from the group and still satisfy minimum requirements. Hence, he developed the following decision packages:

Product X planning (1 of 3): cost—$45,000
Four planners required for minimum planning support and coordination between marketing and manufacturing, and for establishing production schedules and making reports. Would reduce longer range planning, inventory control, and marketing support for special product modifications.

Product X planning (2 of 3): cost—$15,000
One long range planner required to increase forward planning of production and shipping schedules from 2 to 4 weeks, to update in-process inventory reports daily rather than every other day (to aid inventory control), and to assist marketing manager with customers who need special product modifications. (Current level of staffing.)

Product X planning (3 of 3): cost—$15,000
One operations research analyst required to evaluate optimal length of production run versus optimal inventory levels by color and size of product. (Savings of 1% in production cost or a reduction cost of 5% in inventory level would offset this added cost.)

In this example, the minimum level identified (in package 1 of 3) required one man less than the current operating level; package 3 of 3 brought the production planning staff to one man more than the current level. If the alternative to combine the production planning for products X, Y, Z had been chosen, packages for several levels of effort could have been developed for this centralized production planning activity.

For most functions, different levels of effort should be possible. By developing these levels as separate packages, the production planning manager is stating that he thinks all levels deserve serious consideration within realistic funding expectations, but he is identifying these possible levels of effort and leaving it to higher management to make trade-offs among functions and levels of effort within each function. Management can now eliminate the production planning department by disapproving all decision packages (leaving it to the line foremen to do their own planning); or approve package 1 (cost—$45,000), packages 1 and 2 (cost—$60,000), or all packages (cost—$75,000).

In a few instances, different levels of effort are not realistic because of the specific circumstances involved. In these cases, there should be only one decision package at the recommended level of effort, with an explanation of why that one level was the only realistic possibility. In the preceding example, a specific level of production planning effort might have been established by the manufacturing manager for product X if he thought that any possible cost reductions or changes from the specified production planning effort were of minor consideration compared to the resulting production problems or increased manufacturing costs. (However, most managers cannot make such an assessment until the consequences of different levels of effort have been explored, which is done formally in the decision packages. If a manager then realizes that the consequences of a lower level of effort far outweigh the cost savings, he can merely give a high priority to several or all packages for that activity.)

Separate decision packages would not be prepared for each different way of performing the same activity as well as for each different level of effort for performing the activity, since we do not want to double-count each activity and its associated costs. If it is determined that several levels of effort are possible, a separate package will be prepared for the minimum level as well as separate packages for each increment— that is, separate packages for product X planning (1 of 3), product X planning (2 of 3), and product X planning (3 of 3). The recommended way for performing each package will be displayed on that package, with the recommended way usually being the same for all levels of effort for a specific activity.

Needless to say, decision packages cannot be prepared in a vacuum. Planning assumptions and guidelines concerning direction and purpose must be provided by the higher level managers to the lower level managers before they can develop their packages. Managers preparing packages should also discuss their alternatives and recommendations with those affected by their function before developing the packages. In the preceding example, the production planning decision packages should have been prepared after discussions with the manufacturing and marketing managers whose work is affected by the type and quality of production planning.

The minimum level decision package for production planning is shown in Exhibit 1-3, which illustrates the one-page decision package format used by Texas Instruments. This basic format was established to force each manager to perform a detailed analysis of his function(s)—including alternatives, cost trends, and operating ratios—to show work loads and effectiveness, and then to display his analysis and recommendations on these forms. Although separate decision packages are prepared for the additional levels of effort—(2 of 3) and (3 of 3)—these packages

Exhibit 1-3

DECISION PACKAGE [$000] TI-14378-A

PACKAGE NAME	MANAGER	RANKING
Product X Planning (1 of 3)	John Doe	2

STATEMENT OF PROGRAM AND GOALS

Provide minimum level of planning effort for 5 million units of product X.
Maintain updated production and shipping schedules for two weeks in advance
  (currently maintaining schedules four weeks in advance).
Provide finished goods inventory level reports daily and in process inventory
  reports every other day (currently being done daily).
Maintain perpetual inventory system (computerized) on raw material to
  maintain a two weeks supply on hand and a two weeks supply on order.

IMPROVEMENTS   Reduce overtime and clerical effort due to perpetual inventory system.
INCLUDED
                      Replace professional with clerk.

BENEFITS

Activity required for minimum maintenance of planning
function to deliver products on schedule.

OPERATING RATIOS	1969	1970	1971
$ M NSB/planner	3.75	3.60	5.25
Avg inventory/M NSB	10%	12%	12%
Package cost/NSB	.30%	.33%	.21%
Package cost/GPM	.90%	1.1%	.75%

ALTERNATIVES AND CONSEQUENCES

-Elimination of planners would force line foremen to do their own planning (zero incremental cost for foremen); but excessive inventories, inefficient production runs, and
  delayed shipments would result in excessive sales loss.

-Combine production planning for departments X, Y, and Z.

-Package 2 of 3 ($15,000): add back long range planner.

-Package 3 of 3 ($15,000): add operations research analyst.

RESOURCES EXPENSE/PEOPLE	1969	1970					1971					Δ70-71
	TOTAL	1 Q	2 Q	3 Q	4 Q	TOTAL	1 Q	2 Q	3 Q	4 Q	TOTAL	TOTAL
GROSS	45	13	16	16	15	60	11	11	12	11	45	15
NET	45	13	16	16	15	60	11	11	12	11	45	15
NON-EXEMPT	1	1	1	1	1	1	2	2	2	2	2	(1)
EXEMPT	3	3	4	4	4	4	2	2	2	2	2	2

CC	ORGANIZATION	DIVISION	PREPARED BY	DATE
205	DTL Planning	Circuits		

11

are summarized in the section of alternatives on the form so that the reviewing manager can see the other levels of effort proposed. The types of information desired on the decision package forms for different types of organizations, and the possible formats of these forms, will be discussed in detail in Chapter 4. A different format for this production planning example, including examples of decision packages (1 of 3) and (2 of 3), is shown in Appendix A.

Formulating Decision Packages. A decision package is defined as an identification of "a discrete activity, function, or operation. . . ." Generally a discrete activity is the lowest organizational level, cost center, or budgeted unit, and often several such activities are contained within an individual organizational unit. Determining the activities around which decision packages should be prepared is the most important step in implementing zero-base budgeting, and is discussed in detail in Chapter 3. In addition, Appendix B gives a listing of activities around which packages have been developed in several industrial and governmental organizations. At this stage, let us proceed with the understanding that decision packages are prepared down in the gut level of each organization, and hope that the remainder of this book will provide enough examples and insights to allow each reader to determine where the packages should be developed in his own organization.

Decision packages are formulated at this gut level to promote detailed identification of activities and alternatives, and to generate interest in and participation by the managers who are most familiar with each activity and who will be operationally responsible for the approved budget. Exhibit 1-4 shows the basic formulation process.

To begin developing his packages, each manager might logically start by identifying the current year's activities and operations. The manager can then take his forecast or budgeted expense level for the current year, identify the activities creating this expense (activities around which he will subsequently develop his decision packages), and calculate or estimate the cost for each activity. At this stage, the manager should simply identify each activity at its current level and method of operation and not try to identify different ways of performing the function or different levels of effort.

After he has broken his current operations into activities around which he will develop his decision packages, the manager can start looking at his requirements for the coming year. It is extremely helpful if upper management issues a formal set of planning assumptions to aid each manager in determining next year's requirements. Such formalized assumptions might include:

Exhibit 1-4

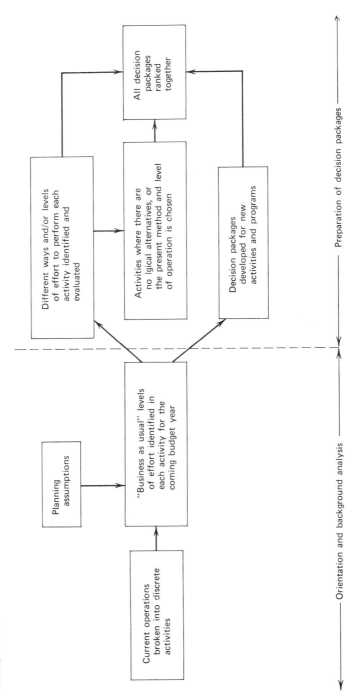

13

- Billing levels.
- Number and types of units to be manufactured or processed.
- Wage and salary increases.
- Number of people served, such as hospital patients.
- Addition to or reduction in facilities to be cleaned and maintained.
- Planned changes from the current method of operation, such as centralization or decentralization of activities, additional scope of operations, and so forth.
- General guidelines as to realistic expenditure levels for the coming budget year.

This formalized set of planning assumptions is needed for several reasons:

1. It forces top level managers to do some detailed planning and goal setting for the coming budget period early in the budget cycle.

2. It provides all managers with a uniform basis for viewing the coming year and estimating requirements.

3. It provides a focal point for reviewing and revising planning assumptions, which in turn requires the revision of decision packages affected by those assumptions. The number of revisions in assumptions can be controlled to reduce both confusion and the cycling of budget inputs in rapidly changing environments.

4. It allows managers to readily identify the actual expenditure variances during the operating year that are created by inaccurate assumptions provided during the budgeting process.

Once each manager has determined the discrete activities around which he will develop his decision packages and has received his formalized set of assumptions, he can identify his "business as usual" levels of effort for each activity—which merely extends this year's operations in terms of next year's costs and requirements, with no change in the method of operations. To determine next year's costs, the manager simply adjusts the costs for changes in activity levels for dependent service functions, for wage and salary increases, and for annualizing expenses of new employees and activities not incurred throughout the current budget year.

Until this point no decision packages have been prepared, but the manager has been going through a necessary orientation and background analysis. The real starting point in the preparation of the packages comes when alternatives to the "business as usual" levels of effort are developed by evaluating different ways of and/or levels of effort for performing each activity. If an alternative to the "business as usual" method is chosen, then, as explained earlier, the so-called alternative is incorporated into the package *first* with the "business as usual" method given as an alternative not recommended.

At the same time that the manager is looking at his current and ongoing activities, he should identify all new activities and programs and develop decision packages that handle them—analyzing alternatives for different ways and different levels of effort to implement these new programs. At the conclusion of the formulation stage, the manager will have identified all his proposed activities for the coming year in decision packages that fall into one of three categories:

1. Different ways of and/or different levels of effort for performing the activity.
2. "Business as usual," where there are no logical alternatives, or the present method and level of effort is required.
3. New activities and programs.

The manager is now ready to rank his packages.

Step 2: Ranking Decision Packages

The ranking process provides management with a technique for allocating its limited resources by making it concentrate on these questions: "How much should we spend?" "Where should we spend it?"

Management answers these questions by listing all packages identified in order of decreasing benefit or importance. Managers can then identify the benefits to be gained at each level of expenditure and can study the consequences of not approving additional packages ranked below that expenditure level. The initial ranking should of course occur at the organization level where the packages are developed, so that each manager can evaluate the importance of his own activities and rank his packages accordingly. Then the manager at the next level up the ladder reviews these rankings and uses them as guides to produce a single, consolidated ranking for all the packages presented to him from below.

This ranking process is shown in Exhibit 1-5. The decision packages would be ranked first by the managers preparing the packages at the organizational level of D_1, D_2, and D_3. These managers would then submit their rankings to their boss, the manager of unit C_2, who would consolidate the 28 packages (5 from D_1, 8 from D_2, and 15 from D_3) into one overall ranking. This process is then repeated, with the manager of unit B_2 producing a consolidated ranking of 55 packages submitted from units C_1, C_2, and C_3. Consolidation can continue until one final ranking is achieved at some desired organizational level. This consolida-

Exhibit 1-5

16

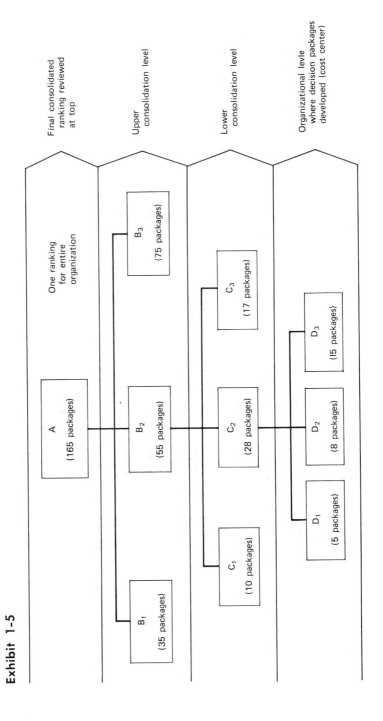

Final consolidated
ranking reviewed
at top

Upper
consolidation level

Lower
consolidation level

Organizational levle
where decision packages
developed (cost center)

One ranking
for entire
organization

A
(165 packages)

B₁
(35 packages)

B₂
(55 packages)

B₃
(75 packages)

C₁
(10 packages)

C₂
(28 packages)

C₃
(17 packages)

D₁
(5 packages)

D₂
(8 packages)

D₃
(15 packages)

tion hierarchy usually corresponds to the ordinary hierarchical organization of the company, but logical groupings of similar functions may be useful even where these cut across normal organizational boundaries.

Theoretically, one ranking of decision packages can be obtained for an entire company and judged by its top management. But while this single ranking would identify the best allocation of resources, ranking and judging the large volume of packages created by describing all the discrete activities of a large organization would impose a ponderous, if not impossible, task on top management. At the other extreme, ranking at only the cost center level is obviously unsatisfactory, since it does not identify to top management the trade-offs among cost centers or larger organizational units, and these lower level organizational units are usually too numerous for top management to make these trade-offs themselves.

One can begin to resolve this dilemma by stopping the consolidated ranking process at some level between the cost center and the entire company. Such a level might be, for example, a division, department, agency, product line, or profit center. The organizational width and depth of such groupings may be determined by four factors:

1. The number of packages involved, and the time and effort required to review and rank them.

2. Management's ability and willingness to rank unfamiliar activities.

3. Natural groupings that provide a logical scope of analysis, such as a product profit center in industry, where the number of packages approved for funding is directly related to profit goals and expectations.

4. The need for extensive review across organizational boundaries to determine trade-offs in expense levels. (This factor is particularly important when deep cuts in expenditure levels are required and managers are forced to make trade-offs across larger organizational units than normal.)

The volume problem can be the most serious obstacle to effectively implementing the zero-base budgeting process in a large organization. Several methods of solving this problem are discussed in Chapter 5. However, the basic solution to the volume problem lies in limiting the number of packages ranked at any consolidation level and properly focusing top management's attention on areas requiring decision making, thus leaving it to lower management levels to perform the detailed evaluation and ranking.

The ranking process itself should be relatively simple, but it seems to be a stumbling block for many managers. In addition to forcing them to make decisions, which seems foreign to some managers, they may have conceptual difficulty in ranking packages they consider "requirements" and may express concern over their ability to judge the relative importance of dissimilar activities, since many packages require subjective judgment. The difficulty and the time consumed in overcoming these problems can be significantly reduced if managers:

1. Do not concentrate on ranking high priority or "requirement" packages that are well within the expenditure guidelines (other than to ensure that all alternatives, cost reduction opportunities, and operating improvements have been explored and incorporated as appropriate) but concentrate instead on discretionary functions and levels of effort.

2. Do not spend too much time worrying over whether package 4, for example, is more important than package 5, but instead only assure themselves that packages 4 and 5 are more important than package 15, and package 15 is more important than package 25, and so on.

The Ranking Form. Exhibit 1-6 illustrates the ranking form used by Texas Instruments. This form serves only as a summary sheet to identify the priority placed on each decision package. The package with rank number 1 has the highest priority; the package with rank number 17 has the lowest priority. The package name, expense, and people information is taken directly from the package itself.

It is extremely useful to show cumulative levels (the sum of the expense for each decision package plus all packages ranked above it) so that if, for example, packages 1 through 12 were approved, management could readily see that the budget for the Manufacturing Support Department would be $564,000. The ranking form used by the State of Georgia (see Chapter 5) is very similar to that for Texas Instruments, but it also has a space at each cumulative level to show the percent of this expense level as compared to the current year's expense level for the department.

The ranking form can be easily modified to include any information desired, but it should be remembered that it is merely a summary form to display package priority and the packages themselves must be reviewed to effectively determine which ones should be funded.

WHERE ZERO-BASE BUDGETING CAN BE USED: INDUSTRY AND GOVERNMENT

The zero-base budgeting process consists of identifying decision packages and then ranking them in order of importance through a cost/

benefit analysis. Therefore, zero-base budgeting can be used on any activities, functions, or operations where a cost/benefit relationship can be identified—even if this evaluation is highly subjective.

Industry

Exhibit 1-7 illustrates the typical scope of management activities in industry, which run the gamut from corporate overhead to direct labor and material costs. Zero-base budgeting is applicable to administrative, technical, and most commercial portions of the budget (some transportation and distribution costs may be part of the standard cost system), but it is not directly adaptable to the direct labor, direct material, and some direct overhead associated with production operations. Zero-base budgeting is not applicable to direct production and manufacturing costs because there is usually no benefit from increasing these expenditures—that is, there is no cost/benefit relationship. The budgeting effort for these direct costs is usually an engineering study with emphasis on minimizing unit costs, with the budget developed by multiplying units of output by standard unit costs. Elements of direct manufacturing overhead fall into a gray area between standard cost budgeting and zero-base budgeting. Some direct overhead costs, such as depreciation expense on existing equipment and facilities, or utilities and power—if this expense is directly associated with machine hours or number of units produced—fall into the standard cost category because, again, there is no cost/benefit relationship. (For these direct manufacturing costs, decision packages can be developed and ranked extremely high if management merely wants to use the mechanics of the zero-base budgeting process to display all costs.)

However, zero-base budgeting is adaptable to all other expenses incurred in industry, even those that are closely related to the direct manufacturing operations and costs. Manufacturing support services (maintenance, supervision, production planning, industrial engineering, quality control, etc.) require an assumed level of manufacturing or production by type and volume but are still variables with specific benefits identifiable with increased expenditures. For example:

- Increased expenditures in preventive maintenance, such as replacing parts before failure, may reduce downtime of equipment.
- Variable levels of supervision can affect personnel turnover and employee productivity.
- Industrial engineering and production planning efforts can have substantial impacts on manufacturing costs.

Exhibit 1-6 Ranking Form

R A N K	PACKAGE NAME	4 QTR 1970 ANNUALIZED EXPENSE		1970 EXPENSE		PEOPLE	1971 EXPENSE		PEOPLE	CUMULATIVE LEVEL ($000)	
		GROSS	NET	GROSS	NET	NX/X	GROSS	NET	NX/X	GROSS	NET
1	Quality Control (1 of 3)	167	167	175	175	11/3	90	90	6/1	90	90
* 2	Product X Planning (1 of 3)	60	60	60	60	1/4	45	45	2/2	135	135
3	Routine/prevent maint (1 of 2)	140	140	150	150	10/2	105	105	7/1	240	240
4	Industrial Engineering (1 of 4)	93	93	90	90	2/6	41	41	1/2	281	281
5	Administration	24	24	23	23	1/1	25	25	1/1	306	306
* 6	Product X Planning (2 of 3)					/1	15	15	/1	321	321
7	Relocate test and assembly					/	45	45	/	366	366
8	Industrial Engineering (2 of 4)					/	35	35	/3	401	401
9	Routine/prevent maint (2 of 2)					/	50	50	3/1	451	451
10	Maintenance scheduler	9	9	9	9	1/	10	10	1/	461	461
11	Quality Control (2 of 3)					/	83	83	5/1	544	544

#	Description									
12	Industrial Engineering (3 of 4)					/	20	20	1/1	564	564
13	Quality Control (3 of 3)					/	30	30	2/1	594	594
14	Product X Planning (3 of 3)					/	15	15	/1	609	609
15	Records and file clerk	6	6	6	6	1/	6	6	1/	615	615
16	Industrial Engineering (4 of 4)					/	15	15	/1	630	630
17	Computerized Scheduling Model					/	10	10	/	640	640
*						/			/		
						/			/		
						/			/		
						/			/		
						/			/		

CC ORGANIZATION	DIVISION	PREPARED BY	DATE
Manufacturing Support–Product X	Circuits	J. Doe, Manager	10/5/70

Exhibit 1-7

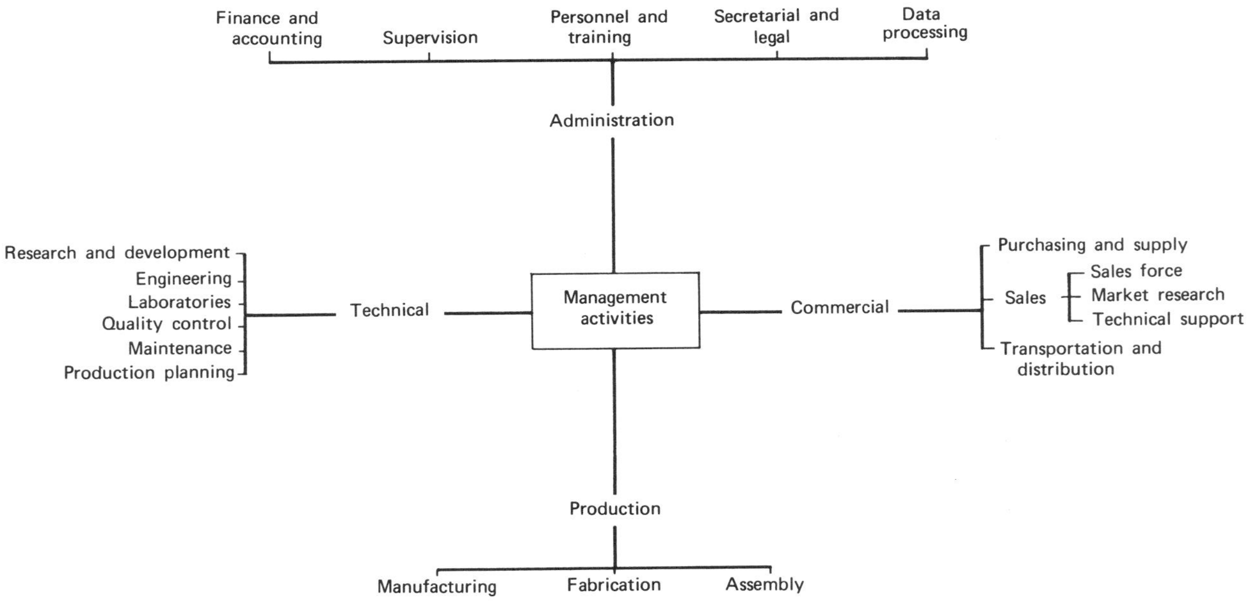

Management activities

Administration
- Finance and accounting
- Supervision
- Personnel and training
- Secretarial and legal
- Data processing

Technical
- Research and development
- Engineering
- Laboratories
- Quality control
- Maintenance
- Production planning

Commercial
- Purchasing and supply
- Sales
  - Sales force
  - Market research
  - Technical support
- Transportation and distribution

Production
- Manufacturing
- Fabrication
- Assembly

Other service and support activities usually accounted for as overhead items at department, division, and corporate levels are justified directly on cost/benefit evaluations. These functions may include marketing, advertising, accounting and control, data processing, training, personnel, tax and legal activities, industrial relations, safety and security, research, and so forth.

Capital expenditures for facilities and equipment are also easily identified in decision package format, with the ranking process facilitated by rate of return or payback period calculations required on most sizable capital investments. Managers also have readily identifiable alternatives as to the type of equipment or facilities available, such as rental of equipment or facilities in place of capital outlay, and can vary the level of expenditures by such actions as delaying plant expansion, going to multiple shifts, rearranging current layouts to make more effective use of current facilities, slipping expenditure and completion schedules, or varying the capacity of the equipment or facility. These decision packages will usually show cash flow (purchase price) as well as the depreciation expense associated with each capital project. Capital projects can be ranked separately, or, in periods of extreme profit or cash flow problems, decision packages for capital can be merged into the rankings for all packages.

Although zero-base budgeting may apply to only a fraction of the total budget in a heavy manufacturing organization, the activities subject to zero-base budgeting techniques are usually the most difficult to plan and control and yet offer management the greatest lever to affect profits. For example:

• Service and overhead functions can be varied significantly over short periods of time.
• Expenses for research and development, capital, industrial engineering, production planning, and so on, can directly impact manufacturing technology and processes and can heavily influence direct manufacturing costs.
• Arbitrary cost reductions in the service and support functions without full understanding of the consequences involved can create severe problems, with cost savings proving minor compared to the resulting production problems and increased direct manufacturing costs.
• Marketing and research and development programs determine the future course and growth of the organization.

Management typically has a difficult time getting a handle on the service and support activities, which are usually made up of many relatively small—compared to direct manufacturing operations—and dissimilar functions that are not subject to the type of engineering analysis used on the direct production costs. Zero-base budgeting gives management an effective operating tool to use in these problem areas, which impact profits far in excess of their relative proportion of total dollars budgeted.

Government

Zero-base budgeting can be readily adapted to all government activities and agencies since government is a service organization that supposedly provides some benefit for the tax dollars spent. Zero-base budgeting was applied to all 65 budgeted agencies in the State of Georgia [health, highway, education, corrections, agriculture, public safety, game and fish, family and children's services (welfare), etc.], for a budget in excess of 1 billion dollars in state funds and approaching 2 billion dollars in total funds (state funds, federal funds, and other revenues).

CHAPTER 2

IMPLEMENTATION PROBLEMS AND BENEFITS OF ZERO-BASE BUDGETING

The type of problems experienced with and benefits gained from zero-base budgeting by both industry and government are almost identical. However, there were wide ranges in magnitude of the common implementation problems, depending primarily on the capabilities of the managers involved, but with some specific problems stemming from the size and nature of each operation. Most of these problems can be eliminated or minimized by effective management of the process so that the benefits gained from zero-base budgeting far outweigh the problems experienced in implementing the process.

IMPLEMENTATION PROBLEMS

There are three general requirements for the successful implementation of zero-base budgeting or any other system: (1) support from top management, (2) effective design of the system to meet the needs of the user organizations, and (3) effective management of the system. Zero-base budgeting is a general system that can be successfully adapted to fit the needs of dissimilar activities and organizations. The many modifications possible are discussed throughout the chapters on decision packages and rankings, and the management and implementation of the process itself are discussed in Chapter 7. The one factor that can effectively kill the implementation of zero-base budgeting is lack of support from top management—because managers experience all the fears and problems of implementation before the benefits are realized. A member of the Texas Instruments Board of Directors (C. J. "Tommy" Thomsen) and the vice-presidents for the Staff and Research divisions (Cecil

Dotson, Grant Dove, Jim Fischer, and Bryan Smith) provided this strong leadership when zero-base budgeting was first initiated in that organization, and Governor Jimmy Carter provided this same strong leadership in Georgia.

The implementation problems that should be expected when zero-base budgeting is introduced can be divided into three categories:

1. Fears and administrative problems.
2. Decision package formulation problems.
3. Ranking process problems.

Fears and Administrative Problems

There are four common problems that can be anticipated when the zero-base budgeting process is first implemented:

1. Managers are often apprehensive of any process that forces decision making and requires detailed scrutiny of their functions for all to see.

2. Administration and communication of the zero-base budgeting process may become critical problems because more managers become involved in this process than in most budgeting and planning procedures, and these problems are further compounded in large organizations.

3. Formalized policy and planning assumptions are often nonexistent, inadequate, or not communicated properly to lower level managers who will be preparing the decision packages.

4. First-year time requirements may exceed the time spent in the prior year's planning and budgeting that used other procedures. (Note the restriction to the first year.)

Zero-base budgeting is a decision making process. Top level managers must make decisions concerning billing levels and other planning assumptions to be used by their organizations throughout the zero-base budgeting cycle; managers must (1) decide which activities and functions to develop their decision packages around; (2) identify and evaluate alternatives and decide on the best method as well as several alternative levels of effort; (3) decide on meaningful work load indicators and measures of effectiveness, and then evaluate their performance against those measures; (4) decide on the relative importance of each package; and (5) establish the budget by deciding which packages they can afford to fund or cannot afford to do without.

The zero-base budgeting requirement for decision making and establishing priorities is viewed as an extremely dangerous and upsetting process by those managers who place high priority on survival, and who have learned to survive by keeping low profiles or "keeping their noses clean." Zero-base budgeting takes away the blanket or security from these managers, identifies exactly what and how well each activity is doing, and forces some very difficult decisions. This fear of decision making and close scrutiny of all activities seems more common and pronounced in managers in government than industry, and seems to be more common in poorly managed organizations than in well managed ones.

Initial administrative and communications problems are experienced in large organizations because more managers usually become involved in this process than were involved in previous planning and budgeting procedures. Some of these new people involved are technicians and specialists, such as engineers, doctors, quality control managers, who not only have never been involved in budget procedures, but who have concerned themselves only with the technicalities of each activity with little or no regard for their cost and cost effectiveness. In addition, there are the normal problems of large organizations in effective communication, in auditing and controlling the process during implementation, as well as in the subsequent changes and revisions required owing to changes in assumptions or upgrading of poor quality and results. These are problems to be anticipated and evaluated before implementing zero-base budgeting, and their outcome will directly influence the extent to which zero-base budgeting will be installed in each organization the first year, and will influence the administrative procedures used to control the process and review the results.

Regardless of these problems, there are tremendous benefits to be derived from involving these additional managers in the budgeting and planning process (see Benefits section); and the need in large organizations for a tool to effectively plan, budget, and control the individual activities is greater than in small organizations where top managers can more readily keep abreast of and judge the effectiveness of each activity. Chapter 7 will address these problems in detail.

One of the benefits of zero-base budgeting is the identification of the lack of coordination among activities and the lack of planning assumptions. However, this need should be anticipated by top management before the development of decision packages by lower level managers in order to avoid the revision of packages affected by these assumptions. Managers responsible for implementing the zero-base budgeting process within each organization need to identify both the assumptions required and any specific studies or alternatives they wish various activity managers to consider. If this is not done, three basic problems will arise:

1. Managers will make their own—differing—assumptions. To correct this problem, we must first find out what assumptions were made and then compare these to the appropriate assumptions before we know which decision packages need to be revised.

2. Coordination among related or service activities will usually be inadequate without a formal mechanism to provide and revise assumptions. In a service organization providing maintenance, materials, utilities, and so on, to manufacturing activities, the service activity needs specific information to determine the amount and cost of service it will provide. A formal mechanism for providing and revising assumptions is extremely helpful to assure this coordination, especially if the service and manufacturing activities are not in the same organization or division.

3. Many managers will not consider radically different alternatives to their current way of doing business, either because they have "tunnel vision" and will not identify these alternatives, or because they fear a personal loss of stature or responsibility if such a radical change is adopted. For example, a manager of a data processing activity in one organization might not consider the centralization or consolidation of his operation with other data processing units, either because he does not know of the existence of these units, or because he fears that his unit will be absorbed by a larger unit, which might cause him to lose his managerial status. Alternatives such as this may be identified to top management when they see decision packages from the several data processing units in which centralization has not been considered. Top management may then require the units to study the possibility of centralization or consolidation, but if such an alternative can be identified before the preparation of decision packages, the data processing managers can be instructed at that time to consider this alternative and save the revision cycle.

The first year's planning and budgeting time requirements may exceed those of the previous year because of the general problems mentioned above, as well as the fact that managers spend a good deal of time evaluating and setting priorities on current activities as well as on new activities, whereas in prior years they had only concentrated on new activities. In small organizations where the span of control and communication is reasonably short, as was the case within each division of Texas Instruments, the zero-base budgeting process need not take more calendar time than the normal budgeting cycle, although more managers will spend more time participating than in earlier years. In large organizations where the span of control and communication is long, such as in the State of Georgia, the calendar time spent in budgeting will probably be lengthened to allow for both additional communication and control time and the turnaround time required to revise decision packages because managers either did not understand the process or did a poor job of identifying and evaluating their packages.

The mention of the additional, time and effort spent by managers during the first year of the process often leads to the comment that zero-base budgeting must be very costly, assuming we were to keep track of the hours spent and allocate costs accordingly. However, this would be an erroneous conclusion because the salaried managers can still do their normal jobs, as they did during the budget period in both Texas Instruments and the State of Georgia, although the additional effort did require some "midnight oil" and weekends—but this is not an out of pocket expense. Also, if we added the time spent in goal setting, operational decision making, and control to the time spent in budgeting, which is an integral part of zero-base budgeting but is often done outside the normal budget cycle, we would further reduce or eliminate any first year time difference between zero-base budgeting and earlier budget procedures.

Following the first year implementation problems of zero-base budgeting, there is a steep learning curve that flattens out during the second and subsequent years because:

- The administration and communications problems are greatly reduced through experience.
- Managers have become accustomed to analyzing their operations and tend to do so on a continuing basis rather than only during the budgeting cycle.
- Directions and assumptions provided by top management become much improved through the continuing analysis of all activities, and the number of revisions required in decision packages and rankings are therefore greatly reduced.

The second year budgeting cycle at Texas Instruments was reduced to half the first year calendar time, which was less than the time spent under the previous budgeting procedures (see Chapter 7 for a discussion of time requirements). The most drastic time savings between the first and second years accrues to the managers preparing the decision packages. Less time is saved by top level managers, who must still review packages and/or summary analyses, establish priorities, and determine final funding levels among several organizational rankings competing for funds.

Decision Package Formulation Problems

Several problems are commonly experienced in the formulation stage of developing decision packages and administering the zero-base budgeting process. Six of these problems are discussed briefly below:

1. Determining which activities, functions, or operations to develop decision packages for. This determination will be discussed in detail in Chapter 3 and is truly a variable, as it depends on what is "meaningful" to the management involved in each particular organization.

2. Establishing the minimum level of effort—demands a judgment on the part of each activity manager, and is therefore subject to question. Establishing this minimum well below the current operating level is unthinkable to many managers, who prefer to identify the minimum level at either the current operating level or, sometimes above that level. Unless there are significant increases in work loads, or a given activity has had its budget cut substantially in previous years without corresponding work load reductions, it is hard to believe managers who claim that their minimum levels of effort could not be below their current operating level.

3. Reducing the dollar cost in the minimum decision package while keeping people at the current level. Managers are naturally protective of their people, yet normal attrition and the shifting of people among activities will usually eliminate the need for layoffs except when major reductions are required. Although such a reduction in dollars without corresponding people reductions is occasionally justified, minimum levels should usually include people reductions. This is because there is often an optimal mix of people and associated operating expenses within an activity, and reducing the operating expense per person often reduces the effectiveness of the people. This problem is common in activities such as maintenance, where a large portion of the cost is related to material and supplies or other nonpersonnel costs; if a maintenance man is not provided with adequate materials and supplies he will lose some of his effectiveness. (When these operating expenses are added back in future budgets, a few more people are often added. Such a cycling of events can lead to an inefficient operation and points out the need for some standard for the mix of people and associated operating expenses, so that people and operating expenses are reduced or increased in proportion.)

4. Identifying work measures and evaluation data for each activity. In many activities it is difficult or impossible to identify meaningful

work measures for evaluation, and once measures are identified the historical data are often missing. At least the identification of meaningful measures usually initiates the development of statistical records for future evaluation, and the lack of work measures on any package should automatically be a red flag to raise the question of whether or not there *are* any meaningful measures.

5. Costing and auditing packages to ensure the proper expenditure level for the proposed activity. There is a definite tendency for a manager to overestimate his costs to allow himself some leeway. However, any overcosting that is not corrected promotes loose budgets and allows the funding of other activities or pet projects not identified in the decision package. It also reduces the number of packages that can be approved for given funding levels.

6. Emphasizing cost reductions within each activity. The ranking procedure identifies cost reductions by eliminating packages or ranking them low in relation to other activities so that they may end up below the approved budget cutoff line. However, activities and packages with high priority also have many opportunities for cost reductions, and the search for these reductions needs to be emphasized.

Ranking Process Problems

There are four common problems encountered during the decision package ranking process:

1. Determining who will do the ranking, to what level within each organization packages will be ranked, and what method or procedure will be used to review and rank the packages.

2. Evaluating dissimilar functions. Higher levels of management find this a problem when they are not familiar with the functions, especially when subjective judgment is required. This problem can be solved by each manager jumping in feet first and getting started. Once familiar with the decision packages and resigned to the ranking task, most managers are happily surprised to find how easy the process becomes.

3. Ranking packages considered high priorities or "requirements." Managers can easily avoid this problem by:

(a) not concentrating on ranking high priority packages that are well within expected expenditure levels, but concentrating instead on discretionary functions and levels of effort.

(b) not spending too much time worrying over whether package 4, for example, is more important than package 5, but instead only assur-

ing themselves that packages 4 *and* 5 are more important than package 15, and package 15 is more important than package 25, and so on.
    4. Handling large volumes of decision packages.

The first three problems are easily overcome with a little experience, but the handling of large volumes of decision packages in large organizations is definitely a problem and can become a tremendous burden on top management if it is not managed properly. These ranking problems, and some effective solutions, will be discussed in detail in Chapter 5.

BENEFITS

In many organizations, the planning and budgeting process is conducted by financial or fiscal people, with only the top level operating managers participating in decision making and formulation of the budget. Zero-base budgeting requires the participation of managers at all levels of each organization. The process was designed that way because these lower level operating managers are the ones who actually spend the money to provide the services, they are the experts in their activities, and we want them to become familiar with planning and budgeting procedures and to be responsible for evaluating their own cost effectiveness. Also, top management should have the benefit of their recommendations and analyses. Therefore, the major benefits of zero-base budgeting result from the harnessing of the thoughts and talents of managers throughout each organization.
    The benefits that each organization can realize from zero-base budgeting can be divided into three general categories:

1. Improved plans and budgets.
2. Follow-on benefits (realized during the operating year).
3. Developing the management team.

Improved Plans and Budgets

The most immediate benefits gained from zero-base budgeting, and the prime purpose of instituting this process, are improved plans and budgets. These result because:

1. Identification, evaluation, and justification of all activities proposed—rather than just the increases or decreases from the current

operating level—promote a more effective allocation of resources because managers have evaluated the need for each function and have
considered different ways of—and levels of effort for—performing each
activity.

2. Top management has great flexibility in reallocating resources and
allowing greater budget shifts among organizations because of consolidated rankings of activities and organizations. Further, the identification of different levels of effort for each activity offers the alternatives of eliminating an activity or choosing from several levels of effort
for that activity.

3. High priority new programs can be funded totally or in part by
eliminating or reducing current activities.

4. Combining planning and goal setting, budgeting, and operational
decision making into one process requiring detailed scrutiny of every
activity results in an integrated approach for the total organization in
its quest for the most effective allocation of resources.

5. Duplication of effort among organizational units will be identified,
which can result in elimination or centralization of these functions.

6. Lack of effective planning, and poor coordination among inter-
related activities in different organizations, is readily identified, which
can result in correction of these conditions.

7. Changes in allowable expenditure levels during the budgeting
cycle for major organizational units do not require the recycling of
budget inputs, but once decision packages are identified and given a
priority ranking, this ranking identifies which packages would be added
or deleted to achieve the desired expenditure level.

8. Revisions in assumptions during the budget cycle (billings, services required, etc.) do not require complete revision of all budgeting
efforts. Instead, managers can identify which packages are affected by
these changes and can then selectively revise these specific packages.

9. Planning models or initial expenditure goals are subject to modification because managers can see exactly what will and will not be done
(which packages will and which will not be approved) at those expenditure levels. These models and goals can then be increased or decreased accordingly, with managers avoiding the problem of getting
"locked-in" by models or initial goals.

10. Managers at all organizational levels have the same basic information and analyses provided by the decision packages and rankings.
Having assured themselves that the proper analyses have been made
by the various activities (or having had the packages revised), top level
managers should be able to concentrate more on reviewing the priorities proposed by each organization and establishing priorities among
organizations and less on their own independent fact finding and analysis.

11. Approved decision packages provide the basis for detail budgeting, control, variable budgeting in the manufacturing overhead activities, and the preparation of other documents. Zero-base budgeting does not require any change to the normal accounting or control procedures, it strengthens the data base and evaluation process from which these detailed documents are prepared, and it may result in the elimination of some procedures without any loss of control. (In the Staff and Research divisions of Texas Instruments, one such elimination was the requirement that all cost centers prepare a detail budget by chart of accounts. This elimination was possible because of the additional analysis and control provided by zero-base budgeting.)

12. Identification to top management of the workloads and costs imposed by general policies, procedures, information requirements, legal requirements (in government), and so forth, helps top management take action to remove or alleviate the constraints imposed upon the operating managers. Managers are sometimes constrained by general policies and procedures that affect several organizations, and over which they have no direct control. Instead, they should be encouraged to develop their decision packages and rankings on merit alone, highlighting any recommended changes—such as in policy—to top management. Top management is often unaware of problems and costs associated with specific policies and procedures, or of information requirements imposed on the operating managers, and is usually eager to make any justified changes.

Follow-on Benefits

After the budgeting cycle is completed, and each organization enters into the operating year for which it has just completed its zero-base budgeting, there are several follow-on benefits that managers can realize:

1. Managers have a tendency to continue to evaluate in detail their operations, efficiency, and cost effectiveness—not only during the budget cycle, but during the operating year as well. Although zero-base budgeting does not require this continuous evaluation, it is common for managers to initiate studies and improvements during the operating year because they know the process will be repeated the next year, and hopefully zero-base budgeting trains managers to continually think along the lines of the analyses that the process requires.

2. Managers can be measured against the goals, performance, and benefits to which they committed themselves, as identified in the de-

cision packages and in their budgets. At Texas Instruments, about mid-way through the operating year a formal set of reviews was usually used to follow up on the progress, problems, and modifications or additions to the approved set of decision packages. These reviews also served as a good preview to the planning and budgeting cycle that began again two to three months later.

3. The ranked list of approved decision packages can be used during the operating year as a starting point to pinpoint activities to be reduced or expanded if allowable expenditure levels change. To reduce costs, managers can continue up the ranked list of packages (from the point where the budget cutoff was established) until they have identified enough packages to delete to provide the savings required.

4. Activities that are poorly operated and managed are readily identified throughout the zero-base budgeting process and any follow-up reviews, and top management can take whatever action is necessary to eliminate these problems.

Developing the Management Team

Zero-base budgeting is also an educational process that can promote the development of the management team. The identification and evaluation of each activity in the manner required by the decision package ranking processes can become an ingrained thought process, where managers evaluate their planning, operations, efficiency, and cost effectiveness on a continuous basis. Managers may also serve on committees that rank multiorganization decision packages, which produces an understanding of other activities and problems. This type of participation in the Staff and Research divisions of Texas Instruments produced a willingness in managers to reduce their own budget levels in order to fund priority activities in other organizations, thereby achieving the common goal of increasing profits by reducing costs, and also producing a better working relationship among organizations during the operating year.

Managers preparing decision packages were also encouraged to have their people participate in identifying and evaluating alternatives, workload measures, and the effectiveness of their operations. In the decision package example (Ex. 3-1, p. 42) of Georgia's Highway Patrol, 45 sergeants from the 45 Highway Patrol posts throughout the state participated—with their Headquarters Staff—in a detailed study and evaluation of how the State Troopers spent their time, and developed recommendations to greatly improve the effectiveness of the State Highway Patrol at a substantial savings to the state. This type of active participation by managers and their subordinates at low levels in each organization, along with review and analysis by upper management levels, can achieve a high level of commitment and understanding for the approved activities, can develop a feeling of working together for the betterment of the entire organization rather than of each manager and his subordinates being interested only in their immediate spheres of responsibility.

CONCLUSION

In most organizations the benefits identified can be readily achieved and the problems can be effectively minimized so that even in the first year the sometimes painful process of decision making proves well worth the effort. However, this sometimes painful first year is followed by a zero-base budgeting process that produces much improved identification and analysis of activities and alternatives, with less time and effort expended because managers know the process and have started to orient their thinking to where the analysis of alternatives, costs, and priorities is standard practice.

Zero-base budgeting is a tool. It cannot be expected to solve all management's problems—which only management itself can do. What zero-base budgeting can do, however, is provide a tool to efficiently identify and evaluate activities and their related problems so that management can make decisions, take action to solve those problems, and effectively allocate and utilize the organization's resources.

CHAPTER 3

WHERE SHOULD DECISION PACKAGES BE DEVELOPED?

The first step in the implementation of zero-base budgeting is to determine where decision packages should be developed within each organization. This first step will identify the managers who will be involved in the preparation of decision packages and determine the organizational levels through which the ranking process will proceed. Each organization must decide for itself what is meaningful and feasible. This chapter is to aid managers to take this first step for their own organizations. To this end, this chapter has been broken into three segments that include or discuss the following:

1. Two examples of decision packages taken from different organizations and activities to illustrate the types of analyses that each manager went through to develop his packages, and to show the variance in the types of packages that are meaningful for different activities.
2. Four considerations that influence where decision packages are prepared.
3. Various subjects of decision packages.

The first two examples—of laboratory testing and of the Georgia State Highway Patrol—are taken from state government and illustrate the wide variation in what is a meaningful decision package to any given organization. The segment on subjects of decision packages contains examples from industry, including an example on marketing, accounting and control, data processing, systems development, quality control, and capital expenditures. Appendix B gives a listing of activities that may also be helpful in determining where decision packages should be developed.

EXAMPLES OF DECISION PACKAGES

Laboratory Testing

The following example of the Georgia Air Quality Laboratory (Department of Air Quality Control) illustrates the type of analysis that each manager needs to make in order to prepare his decision packages. This example would parallel the analysis of a laboratory testing facility in industry, which would evaluate the impact of various levels of testing on research, quality control, or other activities for which the testing service was provided.

Situation. The Air Quality Laboratory tests air samples collected by field engineers throughout Georgia. It identifies and evaluates pollutants by type and volume, then provides reports and analyses to the field engineers. The manager involved made the typical two-part analysis. Part 2 follows the explanation of part 1, which is immediately below.

1. *Different ways of performing the same function.*
(a) *Recommended decision package.* Use a centralized laboratory in Atlanta to conduct all tests (cost—$246,000). This expenditure would allow 75,000 tests and would determine the air quality for 90% of the population (leaving unsampled only rural areas with little or no pollution problem).
(b) *Alternatives not recommended.*
• Contract testing to Georgia Tech (cost—$450,000). The $6 per test charged by Georgia Tech exceeds the $246,000 cost for doing the same work in the Air Quality Laboratory, and the quality of the testing is equal.
• Conduct all testing at regional locations (cost—$590,000). Cost $590,000 the first year due to setup cost and purchase of duplicate equipment, with a $425,000 running rate in subsequent years. Many labs would be staffed at a minimum level, with less than full utilization of people and equipment.
• Conduct tests in Central Laboratory for special pollutants only, which require special qualifications for people and equipment, and conduct routine tests in regional centers (cost—$400,000). This higher cost is created because regional centers have less than full workloads for people and equipment.

The recommended way of performing this laboratory function was chosen because the alternatives did not offer any additional advantages and were more expensive. The manager therefore recommended the level of 75,000 tests, at $246,000.

Once he had defined the basic alternatives and selected the one he considered best, he completed his analysis by describing different levels of effort for his chosen alternative. For the recommended Central Laboratory in Atlanta, the Air Quality Laboratory manager described and evaluated decision packages that called for different levels of effort for air quality tests. In this case, the manager believed that he could reduce the level of testing to 37,300 samples and still satisfy the minimum requirements of the field engineers who used his services. Therefore, he completed his analysis (part 2) by identifying the minimum level and additional levels of effort for his recommended way of performing the testing as follows:

2. *Different levels of effort of performing the function.*
(a) Air Quality Laboratory (1 of 3), cost—$140,000. Minimum package: Test 37,300 samples, determining air quality for only five urban areas with the worst pollution (covering 70% of the population).

(b) Air Quality Laboratory (2 of 3), cost—$61,000. Test 17,700 additional samples (totaling 55,000, which is the current level), determining air quality for five additional problem urban areas plus eight counties chosen on the basis of worst pollution (covering 80% of the population).

(c) Air Quality Laboratory (3 of 3), cost—$45,000. Test 20,000 additional samples (totaling 75,000), determining air quality for 90% of the population, and leaving only rural areas with little or no pollution problems unsampled.

The Air Quality Laboratory manager thus prepared three decision packages (1 of 3, 2 of 3, and 3 of 3). The package form for this example is shown in Chapter 4.

Georgia State Highway Patrol

The Georgia State Department of Public Safety includes the Highway Patrol, Bureau of Investigation, crime laboratory, Department of Motor Vehicles (drivers' license issuing, revocation, and suspension), motor vehicle inspection, safety education, and the State Police Academy. The Georgia State Highway Patrol is charged with the responsibility of patrolling the roads and highways throughout the state; of detecting, investigating, and apprehending those committing criminal acts; and of safeguarding the lives and property of the public. This function is performed by operating 45 patrol posts 365 days per year, with 631 people authorized in FY (Fiscal Year) 1972. The working time spent by these people falls into four categories:

- Operating station: radio and dispatching, administration, maintenance.
- Obligated service: responding to accidents and emergencies, court appearances.
- Other service: training, prisoner pickup.
- Preventive patrol: patrolling rural and public roads.

Costs include salaries; purchasing, operating, and maintaining cars; and operating patrol posts.

In deciding where to develop decision packages for the Highway Patrol, three basic alternatives were considered:

1. A series of decision packages for the Highway Patrol as a whole.
2. A series of decision packages for each patrol post, with a combination of functions in each package.
3. A series of decision packages for each function performed at each patrol post.

The Highway Patrol decided that the best alternative (at least for the first year) was to develop a summary series of packages for the Highway Patrol as a whole, since each post performs the same basic function, and thus to obtain the best results in the limited time available by avoiding the volume and management problems involved in developing packages at each post. The sergeants managing each post did a detailed analysis of how money was spent and how the troopers spent their time, and participated in group meetings to discuss problems and ways to improve effectiveness. Their findings and recommendations were summarized in a set of five decision packages prepared by an administrative staff. (Many agencies in Georgia prepared packages at administrative levels the first year, a few with little or no participation by field people. Most agencies will go much deeper into their field operations in subsequent years, with more participation by field managers in the analysis and preparation of packages.)

Exhibit 3-1 shows excerpts from the package submitted by the Georgia State Department of Public Safety for the State Highway Patrol (see Chapter 4 for the total format of the packages used). Several things should be noted about this example:

1. *Increased effectiveness.*
- Costs were reduced with no change in service by replacing troopers with clerk dispatchers or radio operators to perform office duty.
- Obligated and other service hours were reduced (as nonproductive duties) and preventive patrol time was increased. The improvements identified to increase preventive patrol were implemented in FY 1972 rather than waiting for FY 1973, and the gradual replacement of troopers with clerk dispatchers was accomplished through trooper turnover. [These decision packages were developed in May and June, 1971, which was the end of FY 1971 (July 1970–June 1971). The FY 1972 (July 1971–June 1972) dollars and people shown are the budget figures for the year about to begin, with the FY 1973 budget requests identified in these decision packages.]
- This example shows an improvement in both cost and effectiveness. If all five packages were approved in FY 1973 there would be a 90% increase in preventive patrol time at a 16% cost increase over FY 1971. During this time there was probably a 10% inflation factor, which makes the improvement even more dramatic.

2. *Different ways of performing the activity.*
- There appear to be no meaningful alternatives identified, nor does it seem feasible to eliminate the Highway Patrol.
- All packages do not have meaningful alternatives—that is, different ways of performing the function and/or different levels of effort.

3. *Minimum level of effort.*
This package is, by definition, the minimum level of effort. In reviewing this package as a budget analyst, one might point out that the preventive patrol time in FY 1973 exceeds that of FY 1971, which might indicate that the minimum level could be reduced to or below the 1971 level—thus reducing the people and dollars even further. However, the Director of Public Safety and the Governor did not want to consider any further reduction because of the increasing road mileage to be patrolled and the increased services required because of high accident and crime rates.

4. *Ranking different levels of effort.*
Package (1 of 5) was ranked number 1 of the 111 packages submitted by the Department of Public Safety. Separate decision packages were prepared for packages (2 of 5) through (5 of 5), which were ranked numbers 77, 86, 92, and 96, respectively.

5. *Size of each decision package.*
- The minimum level of effort package (1 of 5) of over $7 million was 35% of the total funds requested in the 111 decision packages submitted by the Department of Public Safety.

Exhibit 3-1 Georgia State Highway Patrol Decision Package

(1) Package Name

Georgia State Highway Patrol–Field Operation (1 of 5)

(6) Statement of Purpose

To patrol the rural and public roads and highways throughout the State, to prevent, detect and investigate criminal acts, and to arrest and apprehend those charged with committing criminal offenses appertaining thereto, and to safeguard the lives and property of the public.

(7) Description of Actions (Operations)

Patrol the rural roads of the State and respond to civil unrest. Operate 45 patrol posts 365 days per year; utilizing a staff of 64 radio-operators, 45 clerk dispatchers, 45 sergeants, 45 corporals and 382 troopers for a total staff of 581.

- Replace 47 trooper positions with clerk dispatchers or radio operators to perform office duty, at a savings of $180 thousand.

- Reduce obligated and other service hours (for example: putting mail boxes at each station, rather than having 45 troopers spend one hour each day picking up the mail from the post office, saves 16 thousand man hours per year)—implement in FY 1972 rather than waiting until FY 1973.

- Increase preventative patrol 14% over the FY 1971 level.

(8) Achievements from Actions

Troopers already patrolling the roads can react faster to accidents and emergencies than if they were performing their other duties. The increased free patrol time will improve trooper service, plus reduce the time required by troopers to answer emergency calls—thus increasing even more the free patrol time available.

(9) Consequences of not Approving Package

The State would not have a patrol force to patrol the rural areas nor would local law enforcement agencies have access to a statewide law enforcement communication network.

(10) Quantitative Package Measures	FY 1971	FY 1972	FY 1973
Operate Station Hours	280	286	286
Obligated Service Hours	191	163	163
Other Service Hours	175	113	113
Preventive Patrol Hours	526	703	600
Total Hours Available	1172	1265	1162
(Hours in thousands)			

(11) Resources Required ($ in Thousands)	FY 1971	FY 1972	FY 1973	% FY 73/72
Operational	7005	7846	7131	91
Grants				
Capital Outlay	110			
Lease Rentals				
Total	7115	7846	7131	91
People (Positions)	586	631	581	92

Exhibit 3-1 (Continued)

(12) Alternatives (Different Levels of Effort) and Cost

(2 of 5) Reassign 34 troopers from license pickup duties to the State Patrol. By changing the license pickup method, only 20,610 hours of obligated service will be transferred with these 34 troopers, providing a net gain of 49,464 hours for preventive patrol (cost $417K)

(3 of 5) Fifty State Troopers for 103 thousand hours of preventive patrol (cost $501K)

(4 of 5) Pay Troopers for overtime rather than giving compensatory time-off—equivalent to 20 troopers, provides 41,229 hours of additional preventive patrol (cost $173K)

(5 of 5) Upgrade 45 Trooper positions to corporal positions (cost $25K)

(Note: Approval of all packages would increase free patrol time 42% at a 5% increase in cost over FY 1972, and increase free patrol time 90% at a 16% increase in cost over FY 1971).

(13) Alternatives (Different Ways of Performing the Same Function, Activity, or Operation)

Abolish the Georgia State Patrol and let local jurisdictions provide traffic law enforcement in the rural areas. Not feasible because: (1) Local jurisdictions would be deprived of the statewide communication system. (2) The mobility of todays population, made possible by the motor vehicle, makes it impossible for local jurisdictions to deal with traffic law enforcement problems effectively. (3) In cases of civil disorder or natural disaster, there would not be a trained force available to augment local effort other than the National Guard.

• Substantial differences in the number of dollars and people identified in decision packages is common, with the minimum level of effort for each activity usually showing more dollars and people than the additional levels of effort.

CONSIDERATIONS THAT INFLUENCE WHERE DECISION PACKAGES ARE PREPARED

The previous examples show a great difference in the type of characteristics possible among decision packages. This wide variation precludes any rigid set of guidelines that managers can blindly follow and forces them instead—at the very beginning of the zero-base budgeting process—into making decisions as to where packages should be developed. However, when managers first begin their analyses to prepare packages at these predetermined organization levels, they may decide that packages need to be prepared at different organizational levels than originally anticipated.

The decision package definition in Chapter 1 states that a decision package will be defined "where discrete pieces of an operation can have *meaningful* identification and evaluation." But:

• Meaningful to whom?
• Meaningful at what organizational level?

Decision packages must be meaningful for both those preparing the packages and those reviewing and evaluating them. If the packages initially prepared are summaries of several "discrete pieces of an operation" prepared by middle management, top level management may still be able to make a reasonably good allocation of resources. However, unless a detailed analysis of each discrete activity was performed, regardless of whether this detailed analysis was displayed in many separate packages or summarized into only a few, top management will never know how cost effective each operation is, and all the benefits associated with the participation of the lower level managers who actually spend the money and perform the function will be lost. The better approach where possible is to identify the discrete activities upon which we want to base our analyses, develop decision packages on these activities, and then make any summaries required when the volume of packages exceeds top management's ability for a detailed evaluation of each package. (The Georgia State Highway Patrol did not follow this pattern because they did not think it practical in their particular situation, but they did perform the detailed analysis at their lowest operating level with the active participation of the managers at this level.)

There are four basic considerations to determining a meaningful organization level at which decision packages should be developed:

1. Size of operation.
2. Available alternatives.
3. Organizational level at which meaningful decisions be made.
4. Time constraints (accomplishments that can reasonably be expected in the time available).

Size of Operation

The size of each organization and its operations is the most influential factor on how and where decision packages are developed. Let us take an administrative function as an example:

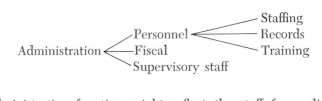

This administrative function might reflect the staff for a division or agency manager who has the line activities in the division reporting to him in addition to the administrative or staff function. The function may be one budget unit if small, or several budget units if large. Under Administration we might have functions such as Personnel, Fiscal, and Supervisory staff (the division manager and his secretary, and other department managers). Each of these units may have several specific functions, such as staffing, personnel records, and training within the personnel function.

If this were a small administrative staff, say five people, we might find their time allocated as follows (in man-years of effort):

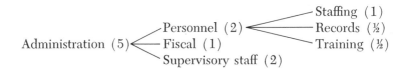

Eliminating (for this discussion) the possibility of sharing people among departments outside administration, or the use of part time help, this manager is faced with the following situation:

1. It is not really meaningful to consider eliminating a fraction of a person. You cannot save any money by eliminating ½ year of man-effort because you cannot eliminate half a man. Therefore, we must construct our packages to show whole people or whole man-years of effort so that we really have a decision—eliminating the package will eliminate the effort identified and achieve the dollar savings because we can reduce one person. (Adding two ½'s is possible, but this would require two decision packages that could not be judged separately.)

2. Limiting our packages to whole people, we could construct the following packages:
- Fiscal: one package.
- Supervisory: one or two packages.
- Personnel: one or two packages on the function as a whole, with fractional effort on each function in each package; or one package on staffing and one package on records and training.

(However, this may not be meaningful unless we can really eliminate a package—i.e., eliminating the Fiscal package would completely eliminate the function.)

3. Assuming that it is not acceptable to completely eliminate any package as identified above, the manager might decide that the only meaningful decision package would be for the function as a whole. He might then develop his minimum level of effort decision package as follows: Administration (1 of   n   )

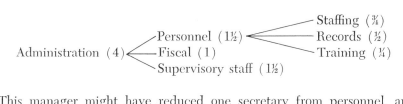

This manager might have reduced one secretary from personnel, and shared a secretary between himself and them. Several additional packages might then be prepared. In the second package, the secretary eliminated in the minimum level package might be added back, with the duties assigned being those to produce the current level of effort for each function, or the same secretary or another person might be added back to perform a different set of duties.

If this were a large administrative staff, say 50 people, we might find their time allocated as follows:

$$\text{Administration } (50) \begin{cases} \text{Personnel } (40) \begin{cases} \text{Staffing } (15) \\ \text{Records } (10) \\ \text{Training } (15) \end{cases} \\ \text{Fiscal } (8) \\ \text{Supervisory staff } (2) \end{cases}$$

In this situation, the Division Manager would probably want the Personnel and Fiscal managers to prepare their own packages. The Personnel Manager in turn might want separate packages prepared for staffing, records, and training because of their size, and might prepare these packages himself or ask the supervisors in each function to prepare the packages. The minimum level of effort packages for this administrative unit might now become:

$$\text{Administration } (35) \begin{cases} \text{Personnel } (27) \begin{cases} \text{Staffing } (11) \begin{cases} \text{Professional recruiting } (5) \\ \text{Hourly recruiting } (6) \end{cases} \\ \text{Records } (8) \\ \text{Training } (8) \end{cases} \\ \text{Fiscal } (6) \\ \text{Supervisory staff } (2) \end{cases}$$

The Staffing Manager might decide he had the two distinct functions of professional and hourly recruiting, and so identify these as separate packages. With additional level of effort packages identified for any or all functions, we would then have a series of packages on professional recruiting, hourly recruiting, records, training, fiscal, and supervisory staff.

Therefore, decision packages from larger organizations (dollars and/ or people) tend to approach "discrete activities" more than do smaller organizations—even if the smaller organization has the same set of "discrete activities"—because of the realistic alternatives available. However, the "discrete activities" should be analyzed regardless of how they are incorporated into the decision packages.

Available Alternatives

The realistic alternatives available to each manager influence the development of decision packages. Commitments or legal contracts may inhibit or delay a recommendation that would normally be acceptable. Contracts for rental space may prohibit moves or the centralization of activities until the lease is up, or the penalties for early termination of the lease may outweigh the benefits of the desired change. Labor contracts inhibit management's freedom of action, and industry practice concerning vendor or distributor relationships may eliminate some alternatives unless the cost savings or operating improvements are spectacular enough to overshadow the problems created by such a change.

In government, individual agencies are often restricted by practices outside their control—federal agencies restricting state and local governments, state governments restricting local governments, and so on (and vice versa). For example, the Georgia Department of Public Health gives grants to the 159 counties in Georgia for food inspection, recreation and parks inspection, and tourist accommodation inspection. On the surface it would appear that we should develop decision packages on each of these inspection functions. However, these grants are provided primarily to alleviate local burden, the dollar amount per county is calculated on a formula based on county population and ability to pay (on inverse scale to county wealth), and the Health Department cannot control how much money is spent in each of the three inspection areas. Therefore, a series of decision packages at varying levels of county support were prepared for these grants *in total*, because separate packages for food, recreation and parks, and tourist accommodations were not realistic alternatives. This analysis did point out, however, that we might change the method of allocating and controlling grant money so that it would be meaningful to prepare packages for each type of inspection, and then vary the amount of money for each inspection by county to alleviate the most pressing problems.

Organization Level at Which Meaningful Decisions Can Be Made

An organizational chart is perhaps the best indicator of the level at which decision packages should be prepared. If a detailed cost center or budget unit identification exists, this is the logical place to start because these cost centers were established initially for the identification and control of discrete activities. Developing packages at this cost center level, however, does not preclude a manager from breaking a cost center into several functions and preparing packages on each function. The previous discussion on the size of the organization illustrates this point. The 50-man administration staff might be a single cost center, when we should break the packages down into the separate functions; or the Personnel Department might be a single cost center, when we might want to develop packages for professional recruiting, hourly recruiting, records, and training. In a few cases we might combine several cost centers into a single series of decision packages, which might have been the case (but was not) for the Highway Patrol if each patrol post was a separate cost center.

Time Constraints

Any undertaking is limited in what can be realistically accomplished in the time available. The depths within the organization at which decision packages are prepared are variable within each organization, and are influenced primarily by the size of the organization, quality of managers involved in preparing and ranking decision packages, and the time allotted (man-days available as well as calendar time) to the zero-base budgeting process. Management can also expect the first year's implementation of zero-base budgeting to take much longer—and have poorer results—than the second and subsequent years. In the first year for the State of Georgia, zero-base budgeting was used to prepare the entire FY 1973 executive budget, with decision packages prepared for grants to counties in such areas as education, health, welfare, and county road construction. Many of these grant packages totaled millions of dollars, but it was not considered feasible to involve each of the 159 counties in the zero-base budgeting process for that first year. At Texas Instruments, there were not the volume and management problems that there were in Georgia, and there was a detailed cost center organization, so there was no trouble developing packages at the appropriate organization level even the first year.

For organizations not accustomed to financial analysis and decision making at lower organization levels, time may become the limiting factor in determining the organizational level at which packages are prepared—because of the time required to develop and rank large numbers of packages. However, in subsequent years, as managers become more accustomed to and trained in zero-base budgeting, they can effectively expand the process into lower organizational levels and handle the larger volume of packages, or handle the same volume of packages in a shorter time. At Texas Instruments, zero-base budgeting took approximately half the time the second year as it did the first year, and slightly less time the third year—with the number of packages increasing slightly each year.

SUBJECTS OF DECISION PACKAGES

After we have initially determined the organizational levels and units that we think proper for the identification of decision packages, and have explained the zero-base budgeting process to the managers involved, we are usually barraged with questions such as:

- What do you mean by a "discrete activity"?
- What are the subjects for decision packages?
- How do you *decide* upon the subject?

To determine which organizational units should prepare decision packages, we made a superficial analysis of activities and functions, but we certainly did not do the in-depth analysis required in the decision packages, nor did we restrict the organizational units identified from defining several discrete activities within their unit around which they might develop their packages.

To start these managers off in developing their packages, we stressed that they had both the freedom and the responsibility to determine what was meaningful to them, and identified the following subjects for possible consideration:

Decision Package Subjects
- People
- Projects or programs
- Service received or provided
- Line item of expenditure
- Cost reduction
- Capital expenditures

However, it should be stressed to all managers who will ever develop a decision package that the subject of the package is immaterial. Managers should be interested only in the benefits achieved for a given expenditure—that is, what the people *accomplish* rather than that the package contains five people, or what are the benefits of capital expenditures in order to reduce people.

These subjects are somewhat overlapping. People or capital may be contained in packages for all subject categories. These subjects merely attempt to identify some points of focus for a manager to consider as he begins to analyze his organization and activities.

People

People are the most common subjects for decision packages because they both spend money and create expenses through their wages and salaries. People may provide the subject in an activity where:

1. Costs are predominately people-related.

2. People perform several tasks or functions and a level of personnel effort can be identified (as in the preceding examples for laboratory testing and the Georgia State Highway Patrol, where packages were identified for different levels of people, with each person performing a series of tasks for a particular purpose or benefit).

3. The functions performed by specific individuals could be consolidated or eliminated.

The following decision package might have been identified by a marketing manager developing packages on his regional sales forces. This package describes the recommendation for the sales managers for regions A and B:

Decision Package—Sales Manager Region A and B (*cost—$45,000*)
Description. Combine sales regions A and B into one region, eliminating manager A.
Benefits. Combining regions saves expenses of sales manager A and secretary ($40,000).
Consequences. Manager for combined region will have less time for market surveys and problem solving for smaller customers, but negative sales impact should be minimal due to sales leveling and expected economic slump for two of the largest customers in region A.
Alternatives.
• Maintain sales manager in region A for an additional $40,000.
• Combine sales regions A and C.

This package might be the only one submitted covering the sales managers for regions A and B since the marketing manager stated that the negative sales impact from this combination should be minimal due to sales leveling and suspected economic slump. However, if there were a more significant negative sales impact from this combined sales region, the marketing manager might have identified his packages as follows:

Sales managers regions A and B (1 of 2), cost—$45,000
   Combine sales regions A and B into one region, eliminating sales manager A.
Sales managers regions A and B (2 of 2), cost—$40,000
   Retain sales manager for region A, rather than combining the managers for regions A and B.

This analysis might also have been combined into one series of decision packages for all regional sales managers, for which the minimum package would include the combining of sales managers for regions A and B along with other consolidations of regional managers.

One common problem faced by managers preparing decision packages is that of how to display activities where individuals do several tasks. This problem is compounded if a fractional man-year of effort is spent on a function or if several people participate in each function. It was mentioned earlier in this chapter that a package displaying a fractional person does not really offer management a decision to eliminate the function and cost unless part time people are involved or the individual is shared between two organizations or cost centers; in most cases, therefore, functions should be combined to show whole people or man-years of effort. If several people spent fractional effort on a function, and the function were eliminated, one person could be reduced with a resulting reallocation of functions among the remaining people.

As manager of Staff and Research Control at Texas Instruments, I was faced with this problem of developing decision packages around people who performed a variety of functions. My main responsibilities included monthly closing (accounting), planning and budgeting, and some ongoing analysis requirements for the Staff and Research divisions. Six people worked in the Staff Division, with the majority of expenditures created by salary and wages, associated benefits, and some miscellaneous computer and travel expenses. These six people performed the same basic functions for different subdivision organizations, so the alternative of eliminating the control function for any one organizational unit did not exist. Therefore, for different levels of staffing, varying levels of effort for each function performed were identified for all staff units. These packages were constructed as follows:

Staff control (*1 of 5*). One senior budget analyst and one accounting clerk/secretary.
Staff control (*2 of 5*). One budget analyst.
Staff control (*3 of 5*). One budget analyst and one accounting clerk.
Staff control (*4 of 5*). One budget analyst.
Staff control (*5 of 5*). One budget analyst.

Exhibit 3-2 reflects the summary analysis prepared for these five packages. At the minimum level of staffing, I identified that I must meet some bare-bones planning and monthly closing requirements. For each additional level, you can see the functions for which additional effort was recommended. Package (4 of 5) brought me to my current level of six people. You can see that my workload was increasing since I was losing ground in the performance of several functions. As it turned out, only packages 1 through 3 were approved, and top management could see exactly what services they were losing for the costs they saved.

A similar analysis can be made for almost any activity. Production planning, for example, might analyze the following functions:

Compiling demand. Customer interface, international inputs, domestic inputs, establishing stocking levels, and so on.

Operational plans. Line balancing, demand balancing, work scheduling, and so on.

Forecasting. Billings, materials, inventory levels, operating costs, and so on.

Long range planning. Capacity and equipment, capital investment, market projections and interpretation, systems development, and so on.

Projects or Programs

Projects or programs are common topics of decision packages, with costs generated by people, capital, and/or other subjects of expense. The following example depicts the levels of effort of a program for an automated inventory system:

Decision Package—Automated Inventory System (1 of 4), cost—$25,000

Description. Perpetual inventory system for in-process and finished goods. Two man-years of programmer effort required for the completed system, with $30,000 for computer charges. Minimum level eliminates ready access capability of system and delays installation from September to April.

Benefits. Reduce production and shipping delays due to out-of-stock situations, and reduce inventory levels by 25% (payback period of one year).

Consequences. Eliminating system would eliminate the above-mentioned benefits and waste the $20,000 already spent on the system.

Alternatives.

• Package (2 of 4): Install system by September for an additional cost of $30,000 during the budget year (cost and installation delayed to the following April in the minimum package).

- Package (3 of 4): Add the ready access capability ($5,000).
- Package (4 of 4): Expand the system to include raw materials inventory ($15,000).

Projects or programs are the only subjects where the use of fractional people (man-months or man-years of effort) are usually meaningful. Many departments are project oriented, and eliminating fractional people would preclude the development of decision packages for each project (although several very small or miscellaneous projects may be grouped into a single package). Project packages may therefore be developed with fractional people, and with salary costs allocated accordingly. Once the packages are approved, there may be some final adjustments to eliminate any remaining people fractions.

Service Received or Provided

Service received may be an appropriate subject whenever costs for services are paid to sources outside the manager's area of activity—whether these costs are received from a source inside the organization or from an outside vendor. Services provided is the other side of the services received coin and may be an appropriate subject if a manager incurs costs to provide a service or benefit to a unit other than his own. The manager receiving services should identify these costs in separate decision packages (prepared by or in conjunction with the manager providing the service) or include these costs within other packages. The following example shows the analysis for a quality control activity that provides service for the Product X Department:

Decision Package—Quality Control for Product X (1 of 2), cost—
$100,000
> *Description.* Inspect 25% of finished goods for product X within 1 hour of assembly completion.
> *Benefits.* Sample identifies repetitive process errors and assures 90% probability of customer acceptance.
> *Consequences.* Greatly increased customer rejection, probable sales losses, and continuing process errors if testing discontinued.
> *Alternatives.*
> - Package (2 of 2): Increase sample to 35% to increase probability of customer acceptance to 95% ($30,000).
> - Reduce sample to 20% and reduce probability of customer acceptance to 80% ($15,000 savings). (Not recommended be-

Exhibit 3-2 Decision Package Summary—Staff Control

Functions	Package (1 of 5)	Package (2 of 5)	Package (3 of 5)	Package (4 of 5)	Package (5 of 5)
1. Monthly closing (accounting)					
• Prepare charge-outs	U	C	C	C	C
• Correct major errors and make standard closing entries	U	C	C	C	C
• Consolidate forecasts by cost center	U	C	C	C	C
• Prepare variance analyses	X-U	U	U-C	C	C
• Investigate smaller errors at cost center level before closing	U	U	C	C	C
• Do facilities-assets forecasting, allocating assets, and so on.	X	X	U	C	+
2. Planning and budgeting					
• Collect approved decision packages and prepare cost center budgets	U	U-C	C	C	C
• Coordinate staff expense planning	U	U	C	C	+
• Prepare decision packages for staff administrative areas	X	X-U	U-C	C	C
• Coordinate charge-out planning with manufacturing divisions	X	X-U	U	C	+

Activity					
• Audit costing of decision packages	X	X-U	U-C	C	C
• Prepare special analyses of running rates, historical comparisons	X	U	C	C	C
• Aid cost center managers in cost analyses, provide control support, and so on.	X	X	U	U	C
• Facilities assets: Coordinate planning of assets, expenditure levels, depreciation, and so on, with manufacturing divisions	X	X	X-U	U	C
3. Ongoing requirements					
• Charge-out analyses, reporting, and forecasting by group	X	X-U	U-C	C	+
• Facilities-assets analyses	X	X	X	U	C
• Support cost center managers for cost analyses, investigating costs, and so on.	X	X-U	U	U-C	C
• Special studies directed at cost reduction	X	X	U	C	+
• Profit and Loss statements for service activities	X	X	X	U-C	C

Legend:
X   No effort, or inability to meet minimum requirements.
U   Unsatisfactory. "Minimum" requirements met; little or no analysis or verification, delayed reporting, and so on.
C   Current level.
+   Increased effort from current level.

cause product defects would approach customer acceptance limits for total product rejection.)
- Delay inspection to 4 hours from time of assembly completion to reduce peak testing loads and overtime ($10,000 savings). (Not recommended because the delay in identifying process errors would cost well in excess of the $10,000 savings.)

For services provided, the service activity should identify for its customers those costs and alternatives directly associated with the services provided, as well as identify all overhead and discretionary functions for review with its customers and higher levels of management. If the service is directly charged to the customer (approved expenditures for overhead and optional functions affect this charge), the service activity's budget will be determined from the list of packages developed in conjunction with and as approved by the customer. In some cases activity levels must be estimated because customers are too numerous for developing individual packages, or they will not commit themselves to any planned service level because of business uncertainties. If the customer is not directly charged for services received, the service packages identified should follow the normal ranking and review procedures in the provider's organization.

The charge mechanisms within an organization always seem to be a bone of contention. Most cost accounting systems have two basic types of cost allocations:

- Overhead allocations
- Direct charges for services received

Most operating managers are not held directly responsible for overhead allocations, but are held responsible for direct charges for services received that are usually shown as part of their operating costs. Although most direct charge procedures are set up to charge only those services where the amount of service and costs charged can be controlled by the user organization, user organizations are often frustrated because they do not have the technical competence to identify alternatives for reducing these costs, and therefore often demand increased services at decreased costs. The service provider, on the other hand, often disavows any responsibility for the volume of service requested and wants to be controlled on unit costs only.

We can agree that the service unit is entirely responsible for unit costs, provided that the user does not place requirements or restrictions upon the provider that affect his costs, but there is also a shared responsibility between the units providing and using the service to determine the level of service. The service unit should aid the user in evaluating his needs and identifying alternatives and different levels of services and costs since this unit has the detailed technical knowledge to make these evaluations. It then should become the user's responsibility to choose the level of service he wants, trading off the services received for the cost he is willing to pay. The identification of decision packages by the providor for his services is an effective way to solve this problem.

At Texas Instruments, the Staff Division supplied many services to the four manufacturing groups at the Dallas site. These services consisted of such items as utilities, cleaning, building and site maintenance, hiring of all hourly workers, telephone service, printing, and photography. During a time of severe cost pressures in the electronics industry, these service costs, which ranged between $20–$30 million, were heavily debated items. To resolve these problems and achieve a realistic budget, each activity prepared a series of decision packages for each manufacturing group and worked closely with each group to further evaluate needs and alternatives. After each manufacturing group had made its final approval of packages for service charges and included the costs in their budgets, the staff service activities could finalize their budgets. (The Staff budget included the total cost incurred plus the charge-out to each manufacturing group.)

Line Item of Expenditure

Line items of expenditure are defined by charts of accounts or object classes. In identifying decision packages, line item expenditures should be reviewed, and occasionally individual line items will be identified in individual packages. Such items might include advertising, travel, moves and rearrangements, books, subscriptions, donations, consultant fees, computer rental, rents, legal fees, and so forth.

Cost Reduction

Decision packages may be prepared for activities of any subject for which the cost incurred is not recovered during the same budget period— that is, for which the cost exceeds the benefit unless we look beyond the budget period. This subject gains importance if there are severe profit problems during the budget period, problems that might cause the elimination of a decision package showing a normally acceptable rate of return, or that might cause it to be eliminated if the future beyond the budget period is uncertain for that particular activity.

Decision packages for cost reduction proposals should show the net cost for that activity during the budget period—that is, the total cost incurred minus savings. If there is a net benefit during the budget period, the reduction should be incorporated into the appropriate package and need not be identified separately. (If the cost is incurred in one budgeted organization and the cost savings is received by another, management may prefer to show the gross cost on the decision package and show the savings as benefits; but if the package is approved, management must close the loop and subtract the savings from the appropriate budget.)

Capital Expenditures

In any budgeting procedure, major capital expenditures are usually considered project by project. The zero-base budget process offers the decision package as the vehicle to analyze these expenditures in the same context as all other expenditures. Since there is usually a difference between the total expenditure or cash flow and the depreciation expense in industry, we can modify the decision package format for capital projects to show both costs. These packages for capital projects can be ranked against other projects and/or they can be merged into the rankings with all the decision packages. Minor capital expenditures required for the normal performance of activities or programs should be included in their respective packages, with the final approval and purchase during the operating year following normal capital authorization procedures.

Identifying and ranking capital projects as part of the zero-base budget process is especially useful when:

1. Capital projects have a long lead time.
2. Benefit will not be realized during the budget year.
3. Expenditure rates can vary.
4. Projects are deferrable.
5. Cash flow problems require trade-offs between expense and capital expenditures budgeted.

Capital packages may identify expenditures related to cost reduction programs—which can readily be ranked on the rate of return generated —or may identify variable expenditure schedules to meet normal operating needs. The following example shows the proposal made for a new chemical processing facility:

Decision Package—Chemical Processing Facility

Cost.	1973	1974	1975
• Capital expenditure	$2 million	$1.5 million	$0.5 million
• Depreciation expense	—	$100,000	$400,000

Benefits and Consequences. Marketing justification for adding capacity; capital expenditure recommendations merely satisfy these needs and identify alternatives dealing with facilities considerations.

Alternatives.

- Delay the added capacity provided by the new facility for 6 months by going to full capacity operation at existing facilities on Saturdays and Sundays.
- Reduce capacity on the chemical storage tanks to minimum requirements ($200,000 saving).
- Slip expenditure and completion schedules.
- Compress construction schedule and incur from 5 to 10% acceleration premium, but avoid overtime and weekend scheduling at existing facilities.

Because of the alternatives identified, especially in shifting start-up and completion dates, we have great flexibility in the amount of capital expenditure for the budget year 1973. Depending on our needs, we could identify this Chemical Processing Facility in one decision package —showing the alternatives—or develop a series of packages at different expenditure rates to rank among other packages.

CONCLUSION

The identification of considerations as to where decision packages are prepared in each organization, and of decision package subjects, should help provide each manager with some thoughts about analyzing and preparing packages on his own activities. Each manager can best answer his own questions about the preparation of decision packages by asking himself the question: "What is meaningful to me for my activities and responsibilities?"

CHAPTER 4

FORMAT OF DECISION PACKAGES

The purpose of the decision package form is to communicate the analysis and recommendations made by each manager for his activities and operations to higher levels of management for review and ranking. However, if managers adequately identify their discrete activities and various levels of effort, large numbers of packages are apt to be prepared even in small organizations, so the package format must find some trade-off between length of document and desirable information displayed.

CONSIDERATIONS IN DETERMINING DECISION PACKAGE FORMAT

The following items should be considered in determining the format and content of decision packages:

1. *Information required to make a decision.* The decision package is the prime tool for evaluating each function and must provide the necessary information for top management to decide whether to fund or not fund each package. At a minimum, this must include basic cost/benefit analysis, as well as any additional information specified by top management.

2. *Type of analysis desired.* By including sections for any desired analysis on the forms, top management can be assured that this analysis is made by all managers. Sections provided for such items as alternatives, quantitative measures, resources, projections, or consequences of not approving the package require managers to specifically evaluate and display the results for each item on every package.

3. *Special and backup analysis (handled separately).* The decision package itself should not be required to handle all combinations and

permutations of possible questions, to handle all the detail in establishing the quantitative measures or evaluation of alternatives, or to provide space for special information required for only a few activities. To limit the volume of packages, this information may be provided as additional backup to each package and either attached to the package or made available upon request.

4. *Additional information required after funding decisions are made.* Special information, such as detail costing by object classes or chart of accounts, final tuning and cost verification, finalizing program structure and assignments, may be done after the basic decisions have been made. If the costs and analyses in the decision packages are reasonably accurate, performing this detail *after* the basic funding decisions have been made can save a great deal of time—managers will not have wasted time detailing activities not funded, and packages can be grouped into cost centers or budget units for detail costing and listing of people rather than identifying this information in each package.

5. *Type of communication and size of organization.* If managers have the opportunity to verbally present and discuss their decision packages to all management levels, the package document itself can be reasonably short, giving only a brief summary of the analysis, with the manager expounding on the analysis and conclusions and answering any questions raised. When decisions are based primarily on what is displayed on each package, the package formats must necessarily be longer to adequately communicate the analysis and recommendations. The size of the organization also has a direct impact on the type of communication used by top management, with larger organizations relying more heavily on the written word. Detailed discussions will normally take place on organizational levels one or two rungs up the organization ladder from where the packages are developed. However, in large organizations top management may rely primarily on summary analyses, and then possibly review the discretionary decision packages around which the final funding level will be determined. These managers may be forced to rely primarily on the information shown on each package because the volume of packages, along with the short time allowed for evaluation, often preclude detailed discussions with the lower level managers.

These considerations indicate the adaptability and variations possible in formatting decision packages to meet the needs of each organization.

The content and physical layout of decision packages is completely variable, and should be modified to fit the needs of the user organizations or even of dissimilar divisions within an organization. Exhibit 1-3 in Chapter 1 illustrates the format used by Texas Instruments. At Texas

Instruments, the largest single ranking was for the Staff and Research divisions, which developed about 350 packages, and top management had an opportunity for detailed discussion of each package if desired. Hence, the form could be limited to a one-page summary. The Texas Instruments form also emphasized quarterly expenditure patterns, since quarterly profit and expenditure levels were a problem requiring specific attention in the decision making process. Exhibit 4-1 shows the two-page decision package format used by the State of Georgia in developing its FY 1973 budget (July 1972–June 1973). In Georgia, about 10,000 packages were developed (each of 65 agencies prepared a final ranking, with one agency having 1400 packages), which meant that the packages had to be reasonably complete since the volume was too great for top level managers to have discussions with all the lower level managers.

The decision package form can be made extremely elaborate to provide all the information ever needed, or to answer any plausible question. However, the inclusion of all conceivable information on the form costs time and money for those managers preparing and reviewing the forms, and can clog the zero-base budgeting process with so much paper and red tape that it quickly grinds to a halt. So we have the common trade-off decision to make between the cost and benefits of obtaining additional information. A two-page format is probably best, as it can provide enough detail to make most decisions. A three-page form is probably about the longest desired because of the volume problems created. A minimum length of one page can be used in smaller organizations as the basis for discussion and ranking. More than one package should not be put on one form since we want to be able to shuffle the forms into their order of priority for review purposes. Even with the one-page form used at Texas Instruments, we found that the additional information provided in the packages themselves and in the review sessions gave top management such a good understanding of and so much confidence in the operations that we made the detail costing of budget units by the chart of accounts optional to each manager.

The remainder of this chapter discusses possible formats and content of the decision package form, and is broken into five major sections:

- General information
- Description of purpose and program
- Costs
- Benefits
- Alternatives

FORMAT AND CONTENT OF DECISION PACKAGES

General Information

General information displayed on each package may include such items as:

- Package name or title
- Rank of package
- Date of preparation
- Organizational identification

The decision package name or title should describe the activity, function, or operation that is the subject of the package. In some cases this will be the cost center or budget unit title if only one series of packages is prepared for that unit; or it may be accounts payable, accounts receivable, and payroll for the Accounting Department. If there are several levels of effort being recommended for that particular function or operation, we have found it extremely helpful to have the name shown as follows:

- Name (1 of n)
- Name (2 of n)

and so on, so that the title identifies the level of effort that the package represents as well as the basic function involved.

The rank number identifies the order of priority the package has among all other decision packages in that particular organizational ranking. This rank number will change from the time the package is originally prepared as the ranking process continues at higher organizational levels, and accordingly many organizations fill out the rank number in pencil.

The date of preparation and organizational identification is optional. When packages are revised, date of preparation is helpful to avoid confusion over which is the current package. Organizational information may include division or agency, department, and budget unit or cost center identification, as well as the names of individuals preparing the package and responsible for managing the activity. Identifying the people provides accountability during the operating year and tells who should be contacted for questions.

Exhibit 4-1 Decision Package Form

(1) Package Name	(2) Agency	(3) Activity	(4) Organization	(5) Rank
Air Quality Laboratory (1 of 3)	Health	Air Quality Control	Ambient Air	3

(6) Statement of Purpose

Ambient air laboratory analysis must be conducted for identification and evaluation of pollutants by type and by volume. Sample analysis enables engineers to determine effect of control and permits use of an emergency warning system.

(7) Description of Actions (Operations)

Use a central lab to conduct all sample testing and analysis: 1 Chemist II, 1 Chemist I, 2 Technicians, and 1 Steno I. This staff could analyze and report on a maximum of 37,300 samples. At 37,300 samples per year, we would only sample the 5 major urban areas of the State (70% of the population). These 5 people are required as a minimum to conduct comprehensive sample analysis of even a few samples on a continuous basis.

(8) Achievements from Actions

Ambient air laboratory analysis yields valuable information for management and field engineers to enable them to evaluate effects of the Air Quality Program, identify new or existing pollutants by type and volume, and maintain an emergency warning system.

(9) Consequences of not Approving Package

Field engineers would be forced to rely on their portable testing equipment which does not provide the desired quantitative data (the portable equipment only identified pollutants by major type, does not measure particle size, and does not provide quantitative chemical analyses to determine the specific chemical compounds in the pollutant), and greatly reduces the effectiveness of the emergency warning system which requires detail quantitative chemical analyses.

(10) Quantitative Package Measures	FY 1971	FY 1972	FY 1973
Samples analyzed and reported	38,000	55,000	37,300
Cost per sample	$4.21	$4.07	$3.75
Samples per man hour	3.8	3.9	3.7

(11) Resources Required ($ in Thousands)	FY 1971	FY 1972	FY 1973	% FY 73/72
Operational	160	224	140	63%
Grants				
Capital Outlay				
Lease Rentals				
Total	160	224	140	63%
People (Positions)	5	7	5	71%

Manager Bill Jones   Prepared By Bill Jones   Date 2-22-71   Page 1 of 2

Exhibit 4-1 (Continued)

(1) Package Name	(2) Agency	(3) Activity	(4) Organization	(5) Rank
Air Quality Laboratory (1 of 3)	Health	Air Quality Control	Ambient Air	3

(12) Alternatives (Different Levels of Effort) and Cost

Air Quality Laboratory (2 of 3): $61,000—Analyze 27,700 additional samples (totaling 55,000 samples, which is the current level), thereby determining air quality for 5 additional problem urban areas and 8 other counties chosen on the basis of worst pollution (covering 80% of the population).

Air Quality Laboratory (3 of 3): $45,000—Analyze 20,000 additional samples (totaling 75,000 samples), thereby determining air quality for 90% of the population, and leaving only rural areas with little or no pollution problems unsampled.

(13) Alternatives (Different Ways of Performing the Same Function, Activity, or Operation)

1. Contract sample analysis work to Georgia Tech—Cost $6 per sample for a total cost of $224K for analyzing 37,300 samples. Emergency warning system would not be as effective due to their time requirement on reporting analysis work done by graduate students.

2. Conduct sample analysis work entirely in regional locations—cost a total of $506K the first year and $385K in subsequent years. Specialized equipment must be purchased in the first year for several locations if central lab is discontinued. Subsequent years would also require lab staffing at several locations at minimum levels which would not fully utilize people.

3. Conduct sample analysis work in central lab for special pollutants only, and set up regional labs to reduce sample mailing costs—cost a total of $305K for analyzing 37,300 samples. Excessive cost would persist due to minimum lab staffing at several locations in addition to the special central lab.

(14) Source of Funds ($ in Thousands)		FY 1971	FY 1972	FY 1973
Operational:	Federal	20	24	40
	Other State	140	200	100
Grants:	Federal			
	State			
Capital and Lease	Federal			
	State			

(15) Projection of Funds Committed by This Package*

Funds	FY 1974	FY 1975	FY 1976	FY 1977	FY 1978
State					
Total					

Reasons:

*Projected if Funds increase or decrease more than 10% from the prior year (FY 1973–FY 1978).

Description of Purpose and Program

The description of purpose identifies how each activity relates to the organization as a whole (division, agency, program, profit center). It may therefore be helpful to provide a separate section in each package to state the purpose of the activity in relation to the overall purpose of the total organization, identifying the goals and objectives of the activity, the problem the activity is attempting to solve, or the service the activity is attempting to provide. In the example shown in Chapter 3, the purpose of the Air Quality Laboratory was to conduct tests for identification and evaluation of pollutants by type and by volume. The purpose was not to reduce air pollution, although that was the purpose of the Air Quality Control Department as a whole.

In analyzing and identifying different levels of effort for each activity, the minimum level of effort may not completely achieve the purpose of the activity—solve the problem or attain the goals and objectives—because of the low funding level. Even the approval of all recommended packages may not completely achieve the goals of each activity because the requests may have been limited due to realistic funding or achievement expectations. Therefore, it is common to have the decision packages of varying levels of effort for each activity (i.e., 1 of n, 2 of n, etc.) showing the same purpose, with the section on achievements identifying how the package partially or completely achieves this purpose.

The description of the program describes the methods, actions, operations, and/or types of people and equipment recommended to perform the package (i.e., What will you do; how will you do it?). This section gives the reader a better understanding of what is being proposed and allows him to ask detailed questions about the proposal, the alternatives, and the costs and benefits.

The decision package form for the State of Georgia (Exhibit 4-1) had separate sections for the description of purpose and program—"Statement of Purpose" and "Description of Actions (Operations)"—while the Texas Instruments form (Exhibit 1-3) combined purpose and program into one section—"Statement of Program and Goals." The first year's format at Texas Instruments had separate sections for the description of purpose and program, but the second year these were combined into the one section for three reasons:

1. The goals and objectives were well identified in terms of product sales and allowable expenditure levels to produce a desired profit, and

the role and interaction of each activity in achieving these ends were well defined and understood. Hence, the additional section on the form did not add to management's knowledge.

2. Managers spent too much time trying to fit the statements of their goals and objectives into the limited space available and ended up with many meaningless "motherhood" statements.

3. The space on the one-page form was needed for other information, and we did not want to go to a two-page form.

In Georgia, on the other hand, we wanted to emphasize the purpose of each activity, and so we provided a separate section that had to be specifically filled out by the manager preparing the decision package. We did this for three reasons:

1. The purpose of each activity, and its relationship with other activities and the purpose of the organization as a whole, was not well defined or understood in all agencies.

2. The description of the purpose helped top level managers in large agencies, who were remote from the operations, to understand the package and orient the activity in relation to the total organization.

3. Planning and policy evaluation was poor or nonexistent in many agencies, and we hoped that this separate section and emphasis on purpose would help solve that problem.

Costs

The evaluation and ranking of each decision package against all other packages competing for limited resources is based on a cost/benefit analysis, and the need for cost information in evaluating each package seems to be the most variable item in the format to meet the needs of different organizations. There are also two basic levels of cost information that need to be analyzed in determining what information should go on the decision package form:

1. What information is absolutely necessary for management to evaluate and make a decision on each package?

2. What additional information, if any, is required by operating management for detailed implementation, reporting, and control purposes (such as detailed budgets by object class or chart of accounts, or monthly or quarterly allocations of the annual cost)?

By definition, we must satisfy the need for the minimum cost information required to make a decision about each package; however, we have complete latitude in putting any additional information on the form. If the minimum amount of cost information is provided, the detailed information can be prepared after the funding decisions have been made. Whichever choice is made in this matter should take into consideration the following points as well as the others (such as length of package) already mentioned:

1. *Advantages of detail cost information on packages.*
- Managers must do some detail estimating to obtain a good cost estimate, so filling out the form may not take much additional effort.
- Top management can have greater confidence in a detail cost estimate.
- Top management can more easily modify the costs of each package (such as changing travel, consulting fees, capital) while still approving the package.
- All required information can be obtained from one document.
2. *Disadvantages of detail cost information on packages.*
- Some packages will not be funded, so the extra effort on these packages will be wasted.
- Detailed information is usually required only at the cost center or budget unit level, whose budget will be determined from several approved packages; therefore, the detail can be obtained for one unit rather than summing the information from each decision package.
- Managers often have some fine tuning and minor modifications they want to make after their funding levels are established, and they would then need to modify the detail costing obtained from the packages.

The real swinger in this decision is the *amount* of additional detail required. It gets very cumbersome, for example, to put monthly cost figures on the packages, or to provide spaces for detail costing by chart of accounts if there are tens or hundreds of possible accounts to use. The decision package format in Appendix A illustrates a detail costing format with a limited number of accounts.

The costs associated with each decision package consist of dollars and people. The types of formats possible can be combinations of the following information:

Dollars
   Major classifications of expenditures
   Source of funds
   Detail costing
People
   Total positions
   Positions by job classification
Time Frame Displayed
   Historical
   Current year
   Budget year(s)
   Projections
   Time periods: yearly, quarterly, monthly

What major classifications of expenditures must management review to understand the costs involved with the package? This question can usually be answered by reviewing the cost reports received by top management, since top management will probably want to see this type of cost information. The following listing displays some general types of cost information that might be included on the decision package form:

1. Minimum information.
   Total dollars budgeted
2. Total dollars budgeted broken down by major classification of expenditure.
   Operational expense
   Grants
   Capital outlay
   Lease rentals
   ‾‾‾‾‾‾‾‾‾‾‾‾‾‾‾‾
   Total dollars budgeted
3. Budgeted dollars with internal cost mechanisms.
   Gross cost. Total cost incurred by that activity, including charges from other activities within the same organization.
   Charge-outs. Costs charged to user activities for direct services provided by this activity.
   Net cost. Gross cost minus charge-outs.
4. Accounting by source of funds.
   Federal funds
   State funds
   Other
   ‾‾‾‾‾‾‾‾‾‾‾‾‾‾‾‾
   Total dollars budgeted

5. Detail costing.
   Wages
   Salaries
   Benefits
   Travel
   Supplies
   Maintenance and repair
   Advertising
   Rent
   Data processing
   Other
   _____
   Total dollars budgeted

Information about people or positions is usually required in addition to dollars when making decisions, and the decision package can be formatted to provide that information:

1. Minimum information.
   Total people (positions) budgeted
2. Major categories.
   Salaried employees (professional, exempt)
   Hourly employees (nonprofessional, clerical, nonexempt)
   _____
   Total people budgeted
3. Detailed classifications.
   Salaried employees: job grade   100–110
                                     111–120
                                     121–130
   Hourly employees: job grade   1– 25
                                      26– 35
                                      36– 50
   _____
   Total people budgeted

The time frames displayed for the above information vary according to the needs of organization, the availability of data, trend information desired, compatability of data, and so on. The Texas Instruments form shown in Exhibit 1-3 shows yearly information for 1969, and quarterly information for the then-current year 1970 and budget year 1971. The quarterly information for 1971 was wanted because of fluctuations in profits and expenditures between quarters; it also provided the quarterly budgets used during the operating year. The 1970 information was shown by quarter because of the major expenditure fluctuations and changes in the level of work force that had taken place during the year. If these fluctuations had not taken place or the information had not been needed for analysis, and if we had still desired the quarterly information in 1971, we could have shown yearly figures for both 1969 and 1970 and quarterly figures for 1971.

Projections were not needed by decision packages at Texas Instruments because most packages did not entail long-term commitments, and midrange and long range planning was a separate function that concentrated primarily on product development and the marketplace. However, in the State of Georgia form shown in Exhibit 4-1, provision for projections was made because current decisions carried major commitments in future years. To reduce the amount of effort involved in making projections, managers completed this section of the form only if the state funds committed by that package were projected to increase or decrease by more than 10% from the previous year. The funds committed by packages varying more than 10% included capital projects, activities in the start-up and growth phases, and programs—such as Medicaid and welfare—for which the population served was changing. For those packages not specifically identifying projections, we applied an inflationary percentage so that we could obtain a total projection for each organization.

One general problem encountered in displaying cost information for activities with different levels of effort was identifying the historical costs associated with each level. It was difficult enough to determine the costs for activities below the cost center or budget unit, much less segment these costs into the varying levels of effort being identified for the budget year (which might be new ways of performing the activity). However, we still wanted to compare the proposals for the budget year with the current cost for each activity. To solve this problem, we adopted the convention of displaying all historical and current year information in the base package. The instructions were written as follows:

If the package being prepared has different levels of effort, the FY 1971 and FY 1972 information is shown on the minimum level package (i.e., package 1 of n), with subsequent level packages showing only 1973 costs associated with that package. However, "% FY 73/FY 72" for packages above the minimum level should show the cumulative level of 1973 expense versus 1972 expense; i.e.,

	FY 1972	FY 1973	% FY 73/ FY 72	(Calculations)
Package 1 of 3	500	300	60%	(300) ÷ 500 = 60%
Package 2 of 3		200	100%	(300 + 200) ÷ 500 = 100%
Package 3 of 3		100	120%	(300 + 200 + 100) ÷ 500 = 120%

This procedure was not difficult since one individual usually prepared the packages for all levels of effort. (The same convention can be used if the absolute difference in cost is desired rather than the percent.)

Benefits

Benefits seem to be the most difficult item on the packages to explain because of the subjective evaluations required. The benefits sections on the forms shown in Exhibits 1-3 and 4-1 are the qualitative sections titled "Benefits" and "Achievements from Actions," plus quantitative sections titled "Operating Ratios" and "Quantitative Package Measures," respectively. The qualitative benefits identified in each package are often difficult to narrate because they relate to the package as a whole. Rather than duplicating or summarizing the narrative from other sections of the package, the description of benefits should identify the tangible results from the performance of the package and identify how the package partially or completely achieves the stated purpose or goals. The quantitative measures vary by type of activity, so the format of the form may provide space for each manager to identify those specific quantitative measures meaningful for his activity. If specific measures are desired they can be printed on the form, or a list of quantitative measures by type of activity can be identified in separate instructions.

Alternatives

Alternatives that may be identified on the decision package form are:

* Different ways of performing the activity
* Different levels of effort
* Consequences of not approving the package

Of the three alternatives, the only section that is mandatory on the form is the identification and evaluation of different ways of performing the activity. This requirement forces managers to consider different methods and allows top management to review these alternatives. Upper levels of management can often take an action to change the method of operation that lower level managers do not see or will not identify. For example, the manager of a small computer center might not identify as an alternative or recommend the centralization of several computer centers into a consolidated operation, because he may not know about these other decentralized computer operations or he may be afraid of losing his job or status if the operations are combined. Top management can also take action to relieve the constraints imposed upon lower level managers if they see the cost involved and the limited alternatives imposed on the operations.

Although separate decision packages are prepared for each level of effort for an activity it is helpful to have a brief description on each package of the other levels of effort proposed. When there are a large number of packages it is helpful to the individual looking at each one to see the other packages proposed if he is to understand the relationship of that package to the total activity. This helps avoid searching through the rankings to find the other packages that the reader may not remember or have read yet. For example, package (1 of 3) would display the summary information for packages (2 of 3) and (3 of 3); package (2 of 3) would display the summary for packages (1 of 3) and (3 of 3); and package (3 of 3) would display the summary of packages (1 of 3) and (2 of 3). Also, top management in larger organizations may look primarily at discretionary packages in the expenditure range around which the cutoff level will be established, and thus may only look at packages (2 of 3) or (3 of 3).

This information on different levels of effort may be omitted in small organizations where the top level of management to review the packages is familiar with all packages. If this information is needed, it can be displayed in a separate section of the form, as shown in Exhibit 4-1, or combined with the identification of the other alternatives, as shown in Exhibit 1-3.

A separate section for "consequences of not approving the package" (the "wet towel" section) is also optional. In addition to not obtaining the benefits listed in other sections of the form, such a section might specifically state the impact that disapproval will have on other activities, identify what legal changes (to perform the activity in the recommended manner) would have to be made in governmental organizations, and provide a focal point for top management to decide whether the cost savings of disapproving the package outweigh the consequences involved.

CHAPTER 5

PROCEDURES FOR AN EFFECTIVE RANKING PROCESS

The ranking process is the listing of decision packages in order of decreasing benefit or importance to the organization so that management can allocate its resources by determining "How much should we spend?" and "Where should we spend it?" The ranking itself, by definition, identifies and recommends where money can best be spent. Management must then decide how much should be spent, and must determine the cut-off level of funding (i.e., packages 1 through 100 are funded, package 101 and all lower ranked packages are not funded). In this final decision, top management must determine both what amount of funding the organization can afford and what packages the organization can afford to do without.

The packages alone do not identify organizational priorities. To make the zero-base budgeting process meaningful, each organization needs an effective ranking procedure to put the packages in priority order. This chapter discusses some procedures for an effective ranking process: format of the ranking form, solving of the volume problem (when management must evaluate and rank large numbers of decision packages), mechanics of the ranking process, and review and funding decisions by top management.

FORMAT OF THE RANKING FORM

The decision package ranking serves primarily as a summary sheet to identify the order of priority placed on each decision package. However, in the review process, the ranking sheet can also serve several other needs of top level managers who may not review every package. Some of these needs are:

1. Identifying cumulative funding levels so that top management can judge the budget impact of approving any given number of packages.

2. Allowing top management to skim the rankings to get a feel for the types of activities as well as the dollars and people involved, and to selectively pick the packages they want to review in detail.

3. Identifying the trend between the current year's effort and the minimum level of effort identified for the budget year (if we follow the convention of showing the current year's expense in the minimum level of effort package), so that top management can readily flag for further review those minimum level of effort packages showing increased effort or no reduction in effort.

4. Providing a work sheet that top management can use to make funding decisions among several rankings, readily adjusting the funding levels during the decision making by varying the number of packages funded in each ranking.

The ranking form should provide enough information to satisfy these basic needs of top management, with the decision packages available so that management can review some or all packages at its discretion.

The ranking form used by Texas Instruments for its 1971 budget is shown in Exhibit 1-6 in Chapter 1, and that used by the State of Georgia for its FY 1973 budget is shown in Exhibit 5-1. These forms are almost identical, with the difference reflecting the types of resource information required by each organization as is in turn reflected in the decision package format. At Texas Instruments, there were wide shifts in expenditure levels throughout the year, so that top management wanted to see the current running rate (fourth quarter annualized) before making decisions. The current rate was readily calculated from the fourth quarter 1970 information shown on each decision package. In addition, we might have added people or any other information from the decision package form to the ranking form. However, the ranking form should be kept simple and is not intended to take the place of the decision package.

SOLVING THE VOLUME PROBLEM

The number of decision packages created in a large organization by effectively identifying each discrete activity, including several levels of effort, could present a difficult or impossible task to top management if they had to review in detail and rank every decision package. Yet management has the conflicting need to make funding trade-offs among

Exhibit 5-1 State of Georgia Ranking Form

DECISION PACKAGE RANKING

$000

R A N K	Package Name	FY 1972 Resources			FY 1973 Resources			Cumulative Level		
		Total $	State $	People	Total $	State $	People	Total $	State $	%*
1	Reviews and Permits	129	129	14	116	116	13	116	116	16%
2	Registrations	113	113	12	103	103	10	219	219	29%
**3	Air Quality Laboratory (1 of 3)	224	200	7	140	100	5	359	319	43%
4	Source Evaluation (1 of 2)	326	204	11	273	253	9	632	572	77%
5	Ambient Air Monitoring	53	43	6	53	43	6	685	615	83%
**6	Air Quality Laboratory (2 of 3)				61	24	2	746	639	**86%
7	Research (1 of 2)	117	56	5	85	56	3	831	695	93%
8	Source Evaluation (2 of 2)				57	38	3	888	733	98%
9	Air Quality Laboratory (3 of 3)				45	25	2	933	758	102%
10	Research (2 of 2)				24	24	1	957	782	105%

TOTAL	962	745	55	957	782	54

*** See Sample Packages.

**Sample Calculation:

$$\frac{639}{745} = 86\%$$

Agency, Activity, or Organization Ranked	Manager	Prepared By	Date
Air Quality Control	Bob Davis	John Doe	2-28-71

Page 1 of 1

*FY 1973 Cumulative State $ as a % of Total FY 1972 State $ for corresponding organizations.

81

all activities in the organization that are competing for the same resources. This problem can be solved by:

1. Concentrating management's review on lower priority or discretionary packages around which the funding levels or cutoff will be determined.
2. Limiting the number of consolidation levels to which the packages will be merged.

Concentrating on Lower Priority Packages

To reduce the number of packages reviewed by successively higher levels of management (where the total number of packages would increase with each successive consolidation), and to concentrate management's time on the lower ranked activities, a cutoff expenditure level may be established at each organization level. Only the packages not included in the cutoff level would be reviewed in detail and ranked. This procedure is shown in Exhibit 5-2 for a four-level organization structure (see also Exhibit 1-5 in Chapter 1). The cutoff level can be established as a percentage of current year budget or expenditure level, or it can be expressed in absolute dollars. (The cutoff level should not be expressed in number of packages because of the wide variation of expenditures contained in each package.) However, the packages included in the cutoff level should be at least listed and displayed at each successive review level to give management a feel for the entire operation; to allow management to verify to its own satisfaction the greater importance of those packages in the cutoff as opposed to those packages being ranked; and to satisfy management that all meaningful alternatives, cost reduction, and opportunities for improving effectiveness and efficiency have been properly analyzed. It takes substantially less time for management to make this review than it does to rank these packages against one another.

Since the total number of packages to be reviewed increases at each successively higher organizational level, the cutoff expenditure level needs also to increase at each higher level in order to keep the number of packages to be ranked by each level within controllable limits. These cutoff expenditure levels must be established at the highest consolidation level first, and then established at each successively lower organizational level. The cutoff expenditure level at the highest consolidation level can be set by taking the expenditure goals or the estimated funding level that will be approved by top management for that organizational unit,

Exhibit 5-2 Ranking Procedure using "Cutoff" Expenditure Levels

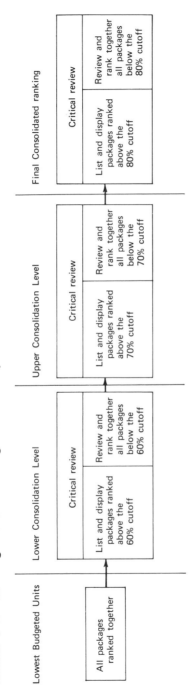

Lowest Budgeted Units

All packages ranked together

Lower Consolidation Level

Critical review

List and display packages ranked above the 60% cutoff

Review and rank together all packages below the 60% cutoff

Upper Consolidation Level

Critical review

List and display packages ranked above the 70% cutoff

Review and rank together all packages below the 70% cutoff

Final Consolidated ranking

Critical review

List and display packages ranked above the 80% cutoff

Review and rank together all packages below the 80% cutoff

and then setting the cutoff far enough below this level to allow for the desired trade-offs among the lower organizational units whose packages are being ranked. Setting the cutoff level below the expected funding level also identifies the least important packages within that funding level, which top management may decide not to fund. Lower consolidation levels would then set their cutoff levels far enough below the cutoff level of the next highest consolidation level to allow for the desired trade-offs among the lower organizational units whose packages are being ranked.

The mechanics of this cutoff procedure is shown in Exhibit 5-3. At the lowest organizational levels, or through several organizational levels until volume becomes a problem, all decision packages can be ranked together in order of importance. At the lowest consolidation level using

Exhibit 5-3

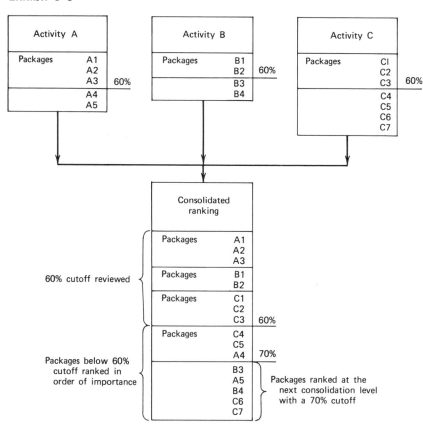

the cutoff procedure, management might have set the cutoff at 60% for all activities (different cutoff levels could have been set for each activity if management had some predetermined funding shifts it wanted to make). This means that management would go down the package rankings until the cumulative expense level for each activity added up to 60% of the current year's budget. Management would then review these top priority packages, evaluate in detail and rank the remaining, low ranked, and more discretionary packages into a consolidated ranking to be passed to the next highest consolidation level. At this next highest level, the packages below the 70% cutoff level for each unit will be ranked together to produce a single consolidated ranking, and this same procedure will be followed until the final ranking is produced.

Setting these cutoff levels should not directly affect the development of the decision packages. The anticipated funding for the final consolidation level will have some impact on the development of decision packages if significant increases or decreases are expected. Such significant shifts should be part of the planning assumptions provided to managers before they begin the development of their packages. However, managers should not be arbitrarily required to set their minimum level of effort for each activity at 60% or less just to follow the cutoff guidelines shown in Exhibit 5-2. It is possible that the minimum level of effort packages for some important activities might fall below that cutoff level on the ranking. Some managers panic at this thought, and claim that some of the packages falling below this cutoff are "requirements." If the managers at the next level agree with this evaluation, then these "requirement" packages will probably fall within the next cutoff level at 70 or 80%. Again, we are only looking for a way to concentrate management's time on the lower priority packages in order to reduce the time taken in the ranking process. If a package falls below some cutoff point during the ranking process, we are not deciding that the package will not be funded (which will not be determined until the final ranking is made, from which top management will then make the final funding decisions), although a relatively low ranking greatly increases the risk that a package will not be funded.

These cutoff guidelines were misunderstood in several of the agencies in Georgia, and some managers were forced to identify minimum level of effort packages at 60% for each activity. Besides causing great panic and confusion, a 60% level of effort was unrealistic in many activities. Most managers then had their second level of effort package bringing each activity up to its current level of operation, so that we did not identify the true minimum level of effort—which was 60 to 100% of the current level of effort. The only time that arbitrary percentages should ever be used to establish the minimum level of effort is when managers will not identify levels lower than their current operations— and top management should take some other actions before falling back on such a poor solution.

The order of listing packages within each cutoff level is arbitrary, with packages normally displayed by some natural organizational grouping. When reviewing these groupings within each level, we know that activity package A_1 has not been ranked against packages B_1 or C_1. In producing the final ranking for this consolidation we can renumber all the packages ($A_1 = 1$, $A_2 = 2$, $A_3 = 3$, $B_1 = 4$, $B_2 = 5$, etc.), or renumber only those packages below the cutoff level ($C_4 = 1$, $C_5 = 2$, $A_4 = 3$, $B_3 = 4$, etc.) for identification purposes.

This ranking procedure allows tremendous trade-offs among organizational units. For example, at the 70% cutoff level shown in Exhibit 5-3, Activity B is still at the 60% funding level since no packages of Activity B were funded between the 60 and 70% cutoff levels, and Activities A and C are above the 60% level since they had additional packages funded. In looking at final consolidated rankings at the 100% or current funding level, it is not unusual to see some activities funded well in excess of 100% and others funded well below 100%. This means that if funding levels are not increased above the current year's level, higher priority new programs and activities will be funded by improved efficiency or the elimination or reduction of current activities.

It is important that these cutoff levels be established as soon as the volume can be estimated so that top management can determine the organization levels for the final consolidation. This cutoff procedure is not usually needed if the volume of packages is less than 100, and it can be used efficiently to produce a final consolidated ranking of 400–500 packages (depending partly on the analysis and staff work done for the managers ranking the packages). This procedure also displays the need for effective planning and goal setting, since the setting of cutoffs is predicated on setting the cutoff at the final consolidation level somewhat below that of the expected funding. If we anticipate the same funding level as the current year, we might set the cutoff at the final consolidation level at 80% to allow top management to concentrate its time on packages between 80% and some level in excess of 100%. If the final funding level turns out to be at 70%, we must retrace our steps and have management rank those packages within the 60 to 80% level that were not ranked against one another. We would therefore have wasted the time spent ranking packages below the 80% level, since their order of priority is not needed if we are going to be funded at 70%. On the other hand, if we are to be funded at 125%, we do not want to spend too much time concentrating on the absolute priority of packages from the 80 to 100% levels.

Limiting the Number of Consolidation Levels

The easiest way to reduce volume in the ranking process is to limit the number of consolidation levels into which packages are merged. However, limiting the rankings to very low organizational levels makes it extremely difficult for top management to make funding decisions since this means either making a large number of discrete funding decisions or else doing the actual ranking themselves in order to obtain a consolidated ranking at an organizational level where they could make effective decisions. There are usually some natural groupings of activities or organizational units that top management uses for analysis and decision making, such as divisions, agencies, departments, profit or product centers, or programs. If volume permits, these units may be used as the organizational levels to which rankings are consolidated, or several of these units may be combined into one consolidated ranking to obtain even greater trade-offs.

If the number of consolidation levels is limited, top management is left with the responsibility of allocating funds among them. Management can make these decisions by reviewing the consolidated package rankings, and determining the funding cutoff in each ranking (this process is discussed later in this chapter). Top management must still make judgments as to the relative importance of the packages in each ranking, but this process takes much less time than merging the packages into a single consolidated ranking.

MECHANICS OF THE RANKING PROCESS

Who should do the ranking?

- An individual?
- A committee?

How should the ranking be done?

- By physically sorting packages in order of importance?
- By assigning a weight or vote to each package to produce a consolidated ranking?

The initial ranking of packages should occur at the organizational level where they are developed, in order to allow each manager to evaluate the relative importance of his own activities. This ranking will then be reviewed at higher levels and used as a guide for merging those rankings. At lower levels, the rankings can be done by an individual if he has detailed knowledge of the areas involved, and may be done by physically sorting the packages in order of importance. Ranking may also be done by an administrative staff for final review by the responsible manager. However, at higher levels, the expertise required to rank packages may best be obtained by a committee. Committee reviews and rankings are helpful when there are large numbers of packages that cover activities with which a single manager is not intimately familiar, and for which the manager wants the recommendations of those reporting to him who are responsible for the packages being ranked.

The membership of any committee is at the discretion of the individual responsible for the organizational unit. In most instances the committee follows the organization structure and consists of those managers whose packages are being ranked as well as the manager they report to who is responsible for that consolidated organization. Following the organization shown in Exhibit 1-5 in Chapter 1, the consolidated rankings for units D_1, D_2, and D_3 would be determined by a committee chaired by the manager of C_2, with the managers of D_1, D_2, and D_3 as members. The manager of C_2, together with the managers of C_1 and C_3, would then serve as committee members at the next higher organizational level, chaired by the manager of B_2. This committee procedure continues to the final consolidation level.

The consolidation hierarchy usually corresponds to the organization structure, but logical groupings of similar activities, or a program or project ranking in which several organizations participate, may be useful for establishing a consolidated ranking even where these cut across normal organizational boundaries. For example, at Texas Instruments the packages for new program development for the management systems (computer) operations for all divisions were ranked together to establish an overall set of priorities for the corporation. Although these packages were also ranked along with other activities in their respective divisions, this ranking across organizational boundaries was used to adjust the funding levels for each division. Because of the varying profit situations in each division, packages with higher priority to the corporation were disapproved in a division that had a very tight profit picture, whereas packages with lower priority to the corporation were approved in a division that had a better profit picture. Top corporate management then used each division's ranking along with the overview provided by the consolidated management systems ranking to make the final funding decisions. This management systems ranking was done by a committee headed by the manager of the corporate management systems, with members consisting of the division managers for each division's management systems operation.

Combinations of individual and committee rankings can also be used. For example, initial ranking might be done by an administrative staff (individual or committee), with a final review and modification done by the operating manager responsible for that organizational entity.

The major disadvantage in using a committee is the added time required for discussion. The additional time required by a committee (versus individual) ranking *may not* be excessive if the individual who is to rank the packages is not reasonably familiar with the activity and has to obtain additional information or clarification about specific packages before he can rank them; it *may not* be excessive if an efficient committee review and voting procedure is used (see the following sections on "Voting Mechanisms" and "Committee Review and Ranking Procedures"). Effectiveness also depends heavily on the capabilities and personalities of the committee members themselves. If the members are willing to have open and frank discussions, and can quickly grasp the essentials of the packages concerning unfamiliar activities, the committee can be effective. Such a committee can also be an effective management training tool and can improve working relationships among organizations as they learn more about each other's activities and problems.

Voting Mechanisms

When the number of decision packages exceeds 50 or so, it becomes difficult to physically rank them. Whether the ranking is done by an individual or a committee, it is usually easier to assign a weight or vote to each package as it is reviewed, and then to establish the ranking based on the weighting or voting. Usually the value assigned to each package is considered a "weight" if assigned by an individual and a "vote" if assigned by a committee. Here, however, we will use the general term, voting, to mean either weight or vote, depending on whether it is assigned by an individual or a committee.

The voting mechanism can be simple or complex depending on the number of criteria to be evaluated, the ability to evaluate the packages against the specified criteria, and the number of packages and time allotted to the ranking process. Three basic voting alternatives might be considered:

1. Each member gets one vote on some fixed scale, with the average or total points used to determine the ranking.

2. Each member votes on several criteria (with even or weighted values), with the total points used to determine the ranking.

3. A combination of 1 and 2, with alternative 1 used for a preliminary ranking and alternative 2 used for the detailed ranking around the cutoff level after it has been established.

The single-scale voting criteria shown in Exhibit 5-4 was used throughout Texas Instruments and some agencies in the State of Georgia. This scale is perhaps the simplest available, was designed for overhead and service activities requiring subjective judgment, and is reasonably effective and efficient when a large number of packages are to be ranked. Each committee member has one vote on each package, with the packages ranked in order of the highest number of votes. Given a list of packages to be reviewed and ranked, each manager can get a rough

Exhibit 5-4

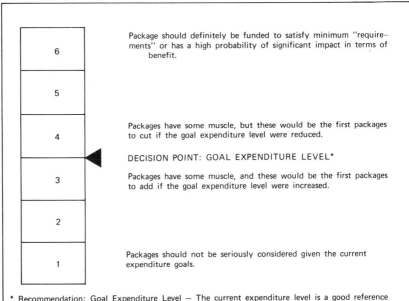

6	Package should definitely be funded to satisfy minimum "require-- ments" or has a high probability of significant impact in terms of benefit.
5	
4	Packages have some muscle, but these would be the first packages to cut if the goal expenditure level were reduced.
	DECISION POINT: GOAL EXPENDITURE LEVEL*
3	Packages have some muscle, and these would be the first packages to add if the goal expenditure level were increased.
2	
1	Packages should not be seriously considered given the current expenditure goals.

* Recommendation: Goal Expenditure Level — The current expenditure level is a good reference point for decision making, since each manager can evaluate in his own mind whether he thinks a new function or expanded function is important enough to be voted 4, 5, or 6, with this additional expenditure obtained by reducing or eliminating current functions.

idea of where he thinks the goal expenditure dollars should be spent. However, since packages are usually voted upon one at a time as they are reviewed (especially when there are large numbers of them), the goal expenditure level may not fall exactly between the 3 and the 4. However, this creates no problem since the ranking of packages in relation to one another has still been achieved, but some fine tuning of rankings may be required around the cutoff expenditure level. We have also found it helpful to have a review session after the detailed ranking, in which the votes of the members are displayed, misunderstandings of package content and differences of opinion are discussed, and the final ranking is established.

The voting scale can have any number of points, with 6 or 10 points being most common. We have found that an even number of points is best, so that there is no middle ground to catch the largest number of packages (e.g., a scale of 5 allows members to avoid decision making by voting 3 on all but the most or least important packages, with 3 catching as many as 60% of the packages and not producing the desired spread in packages with different priorities). With a large volume of packages and a limited voting scale of 6 to 10 points, many packages may end up with the same number of points. If an individual is ranking the packages with a 6 or 10 point scale, a large number of packages may end up with the same weight. If a five-member committee is ranking the packages with a 6 point scale, the spread of possible points is from 5 (if all members vote 1) to 30 (if all members vote 6). A large number of packages may still receive the same vote, but the number of packages receiving the same vote will be fewer than if an individual did the weighting, because of the greater point spread. This possibility of having several packages with the same weight or vote should not create any major problems, nor should it cause management to adopt scales with more points or to create larger committees in order to increase the point spread, since a relative order of priority has still been achieved. If a large number of packages with the same vote falls in the decision range around which the funding level will be determined, the ranking of these packages will need to be refined. However, management does not have to spend time fine tuning the very high ranked packages or the packages that fall well below the expected expenditure level.

Multiple voting criteria, or voting criteria more specific than the subjective scale identified in Exhibit 5-4, need to be tailored to the needs of the decision makers who rank the packages. The criteria shown in Exhibit 5-5 were also designed for overhead and service activities and force managers to subjectively evaluate each package on three criteria as opposed to one. Using these multiple criteria takes slightly

Exhibit 5-5

Each member votes on each criterion for each package, with
even or weighted values for each criterion, with the total points used to determine the ranking.

(a.) Legal or Operating Requirements

Package may be
deferred

1	2	3	4	5	6

Package required to meet
minimum legal or operating
requirements

Reduced ability to meet operating
demands or achieve department
goals

(b.) Big Impact (High Leverage) Project

Package will have
no measurable
effect on pro-
fitability

1	2	3	4	5	6

Great impact potential in
relation to cost in short
or long term

Estimated return of 25%

(c.) High Level of Exposure or Risk

Little or no risk
in delaying or
eliminating
package

1	2	3	4	5	6

Delay creates high level
of risk in relation to
package cost

Probability of risk loss versus
package cost about equal

longer but may produce a better ranking. Extremely detailed criteria, including market evaluations, risk, and the like, may be developed to judge a few highly important packages, such as long range research and development programs. The additional time and effort spent on such decision packages may be warranted because of the tremendous impact that the elimination or the success or failure of each funded program could have on the future of a high technology industry.

Committee Review and Ranking Procedures

The effectiveness of a committee review and ranking procedure depends on the nature of the operations involved in the ranking, the number of packages being ranked, the time available for ranking, the size of the committee, and the personalities of the committee members. Since committee needs and makeup can vary so widely, no single procedure will work effectively for all of them. This section describes the general committee procedure used in the Staff and Research divisions of Texas Instruments, which was also adopted in some of the manufacturing divisions at Texas Instruments and some state agencies in Georgia, and which may be used and modified by other committees faced with the same review and ranking task.

Each committee must first make several basic decisions about its review and ranking procedures:

1. Which packages are to be ranked
2. Voting criteria
3. Method of presentation
4. Presentation procedures
5. Review and finalization of the ranking

Each committee will probably review all packages in detail or summary to get a basic feel for the operations. However, the committee may not rank all the packages but may concentrate instead on the lower priority or discretionary packages around which the funding levels will be determined (using the cutoff procedure described earlier in this chapter). In addition to setting this upper limit, the committee may set a lower limit for low priority packages that have little chance of being funded. Hence, a committee may concentrate its time on ranking packages that fall between 80 and 110% of the current year's expenditure level in each unit's ranking if they anticipate a final 95 to 100% funding level for the consolidated ranking. (This concentration on lower priority packages does not negate the zero-base principle, since all activities were analyzed in detail and no manager was given any funding level that he did not completely justify. Also, at an 80% funding level, individual activities may be eliminated or funded well in excess of 80%.) The committee must also establish its voting criteria, such as the ones discussed in the previous section of this chapter.

The method of presentation is a logistics problem dependent on the number of packages to be ranked and the number of committee members. There are three basic methods of presenting packages for committee review, discussion, and ranking:

1. Provide each committee member with a copy of the decision packages and with ranking sheets.
2. Provide a visual presentation of packages and rankings (such as foils, slides, overhead projectors, opaque projectors, that can project the decision package onto a screen).
3. A combination of 1 and 2.

Providing copies of each package to each member can be effective with a limited number of packages and a small committee but can become an exercise in paper shuffling with many packages and a large committee. The use of visual presentations can be more efficient from a logistics standpoint since only one document is needed for the presentation. Committees might also combine both methods of presentation. For example, members may use copies of the ranking forms for each organization to review the types of activities being ranked and their related costs and priorities, use the ranking form as an overall reference as to cumulative costs and relative priorities during the review of each package, or use the ranking form as a voting form on which to place their votes for each package as it is reviewed. The packages themselves might then be shown by visual presentation. It might also be useful to have one or two sets of packages and rankings to rotate among committee members before the meeting, then to use visual presentations at the meetings, so that complete sets of packages do not have to be prepared for each committee member.

In the Staff and Research divisions of Texas Instruments, four major organizational units were merged into one consolidated ranking, which was reviewed and the final funding level established by the President and the Executive Committee. Each of the four organizations had achieved its own consolidated ranking through two or three consolidation levels. The ranking committee consisted of five members—the director of each of the four organizations and one member from the Board of Directors who served as chairman. The committee reviewed about 300 packages, ranking about 125 packages that fell between the 70 and 110% of the current year's expenditure level in each of the four organizations, and used the 6 point voting criteria shown in Exhibit 5-4. The committee spent about two days in its ranking and reviewing sessions, using the following presentation procedures:

1. Committee members were given copies of the ranking sheets for each of the four organizations before the review sessions.

2. For the reviewing and ranking, each organization was allotted time in proportion to the number of packages to be ranked, and all packages from each organization were reviewed and ranked before starting the review of another organization.

3. Packages were normally presented by using an overhead projector, with the presentation made by one or several department managers within each of the four organizations. (Because of the volume of packages, the individual who prepared each package did not make this presentation. For consistency in presentation, when large numbers of

packages are involved it is usually easier for a few individuals to present many packages than for many individuals to present only a few. At lower organization levels, however, the manager who developed the package often presented it for review and ranking.)

4. The presentation for each organization started with a review of those high priority packages above the 70% cutoff level (the levels for specific activities within each organization at the 70% level varied from a low of 0 to a high of over 100%).

- These packages were usually reviewed by displaying the package and briefly describing its content.
- The committee members had the option to pull packages out of this cutoff and put them in the ranking.

5. Each department manager briefly presented the packages within the 70% cutoff, and then presented his packages that fell between 70 and 110%. These packages were sometimes presented in rank order but were usually presented in some logical functional order for easier understanding.

6. Committee members voted after presentation and discussion of each package. The ranking form was used as the voting ballot, with the members placing their votes in the margin. This was especially helpful in aiding the ease and accuracy of voting since packages were not presented in the order they were ranked.

7. After the voting on the packages from all four organizations was completed, a consolidated ranking was produced based on the total number of points received, and this ranking was provided to each committee member for his review.

8. The committee reconvened to review the consolidated ranking. The votes of each member on every package were displayed, misunderstandings of package content and differences of opinion were discussed, and the final ranking was established.

9. The packages were then renumbered, sorted in order of priority, and the final ranking sheets prepared.

This ranking was then presented to the President and the Executive Committee for final decision making and funding.

The first year this committee process was used, the members did not have a detailed understanding of each other's activities, which slowed down the ranking. However, the members soon developed this detailed understanding, which aided working relationships during the operating year. Members would rank packages from other organizations higher than their own, so that even if they did not get all the funds they would have liked, they felt they got their fair share; the President had to make only one funding decision rather than trying to trade-off among the requests from each of the four organizations competing for limited funds; and a better resource allocation was produced for the Staff and Research divisions as a whole.

REVIEW AND FUNDING DECISIONS BY TOP MANAGEMENT

The final consolidated rankings from the various organizational units will usually be reviewed by top management in order to establish the funding levels of each organization by determining the cutoff level in each of the rankings. Although top management must make this trade-off among several organizations competing for limited resources, because of the volume problems already discussed these funding decisions will usually be made by subjective comparison of the separate rankings instead of by producing one consolidated ranking. This should not be difficult since management has a detailed identification and evaluation of each activity as presented in the decision packages, and with selective modification of these rankings by top management, if required, top management should be able to evaluate the effectiveness of each organization at various funding levels in producing the desired goals and objectives. Depending on the volume of packages involved and the time available, top management may review the packages or may concentrate on summary analyses describing the impact and effectiveness of each organization at various funding levels.

At Texas Instruments, top management reviewed the decision packages, concentrating on those within the 70 to 110% expenditure range for the Staff and Research divisions—as did the committee that produced that consolidated ranking. The ranking was modified slightly, with top management eliminating some packages and specifying that others be funded. With this modified ranking, top management then made a preliminary funding decision. This initially identified cutoff level was later revised as needs of other organizations and the total profit picture of the corporation were reviewed. For these revisions, top management went back to each ranking and merely deleted or added packages above or below the cutoff level previously established. Hence, management could continuously revise funding levels by moving the cutoff up or down the ranking, which did not require additional work or revisions from any organization.

In the State of Georgia, with 10,000 decision packages and 65 agency rankings, the volume was too great for the Governor to review all packages. Therefore, the Governor concentrated on the summary analyses and reviews provided by his financial staff in the Budget Bureau. He had a review with each agency, and concentrated his time on reviewing policy questions, major increases and decreases in existing programs, new programs and capital expenditures, and a few specific packages and rankings where there appeared to be problems. With the use of the computer (see Chapter 9), the Governor was then able to play "what if" among the 65 agencies to balance the funding against anticipated revenues. Four levels of funding were identified from the ranking:

- *Level 1.* Minimum level of funding recommended. If the minimum level were approved for all agencies, the total funding would be less than anticipated revenues.
- *Level 2.* "What if" (tentative) level within the recommended funding range. This level will become the approved level when the needs of all agencies have been reviewed.
- *Level 3.* Maximum level of funding recommended. If the maximum level were approved for all agencies, the total funding would exceed anticipated revenues.
- *Level 4.* Total agency request. This level might already have been limited by some expenditure guidelines.

As each agency was reviewed, the minimum and maximum levels were established, with the impact on the various operations and programs performed by each agency identified. During this review, a tentative funding level (Level 2) was established for each agency. As the needs of other agencies were reviewed and evaluated, the recommended funding levels for each agency could be continuously adjusted to balance to the anticipated revenue. In the final analysis, the Governor could decide to increase revenues, could identify those packages funded by the increased revenue, and could show that these packages on which he was trying to justify increased taxes were less important than the packages he had funded under current taxes. Without the use of zero-base budgeting, major new programs were usually funded through increased taxes. Using zero-base budgeting, high priority new programs could be funded completely or in part by improved efficiency and the elimination or reduction of current activities with lower priority.

The Profit Plan

The final funding decisions for those activities using zero-base budgeting are determined by establishing the cutoff level on each ranking (packages 1–100 funded, package 101 and all lower ranked packages not funded). The previous section identified the flexibility and "what if" capabilities made available to top management by the ranked decision packages. To make the final funding decisions, management must incorporate the zero-base budgeting analysis into the total cost picture in order to develop its profit plan. Management will develop its profit plan by merging the income and expense plans:

Income	(minus)	Expense	(equals)	Pretax Profit
Sales Other income		Direct labor Direct material } Standard Some direct overhead } cost ———→		(fixed)

		Manufacturing service
		  and support
		Department and divi- } Zero-base
		  sion overhead budgeting ←———→
		Corporate overhead
				(variable)

The sales plan or forecast and the resulting budgets for direct labor, material, and overhead are normally the first to be finalized. Given a specified state-of-the-art in the manufacturing process, the relationship between sales and direct manufacturing costs is reasonably fixed, with inventory levels being the only major variable that management can manipulate to affect profits (which in turn depends on the accounting methods used for materials, supplies, goods in process, and finished goods). Therefore, the major variable in management's arsenal to impact the profit plan are the activities displayed in the decision package rankings, with longer term profits heavily affected by the packages approved for marketing, research and development, industrial engineering, and so on.

The corporation's profit plan will be put together by consolidating such plans from many organizational units. Profit plans will usually be established for profit centers, product lines, or departments. These plans are then consolidated, along with some division overhead, into the division profit plan; the profit plans for all divisions are in turn consolidated, along with some corporate overhead, into the corporate profit plan. This consolidation is an iterative decision making process where management can be guided by models or historical trends in establishing profit levels for each organizational unit. However, profit problems from one organization, major new expenditures on product development or new facilities, and overall corporate profit objectives, force top management to evaluate the profit plans of individual product departments against corporate profit needs as well as against each department's profit objective. In times of profit pressure, it is not unusual "to rob Peter to pay Paul" by further reducing the budget in an organization that has already met its profit objective. The flexibility and "what if" capabilities of zero-base budgeting aid management in making these decisions and evaluating the consequences of budget reductions. Management can then revise the budgets by revising the cutoff level on any or all rankings, satisfied that the reductions have eliminated or reduced the least important activities to the corporation, or can revise its profit objectives if the consequences associated with further budget reductions are unacceptable or unrealistic.

Zero-base budgeting provides a systematic process to evaluate and rank projects by priority, which is normally done informally in typical planning and budgeting procedures, and provides management with a flexible operating tool to answer the questions:

- Where and how can we most effectively spend our money?
- How much should we spend?

CHAPTER 6

THE DYNAMICS OF THE PROCESS

We do not live in a static world, and if we are to operate effectively we must be able to adapt readily to our changing environment. Since planning and budgeting procedures usually provide the mechanics for industry and government to make any major operating adjustments, an effective planning and budgeting procedure must be quick reacting and responsive to accommodate change. Zero-base budgeting has proved effective in handling rapidly changing situations, and has several special capabilities built into the system:

- Decision packages can be modified or deleted without upsetting other packages or rankings.
- Decision packages for new programs or activities can be added at any time and merely slotted into their appropriate positions in the ranking.
- Rankings can be easily revised with changing priorities.
- Top management can continuously revise the funding levels (decreasing them by moving up the ranking to decrease the number of packages approved, or increasing them by moving down the ranking) without recycling the budget inputs from the organizations involved.

In addition to these inherent capabilities, zero-base budgeting can provide management with a powerful operating tool to adjust to a changing environment in several ways:

1. Revisions of planning assumptions during the planning and budgeting process. Decision packages and rankings can be revised on an exception basis to conform to the revised planning assumptions.
2. Rebudgeting during the operating year. Major changes in opera-

tions or cost reductions can be quickly identified and evaluated, with a revised operating plan and budget prepared.

3. Variable budgeting. Zero-base budgeting provides a basis to establish variable budgeting techniques and identifies specific management actions to adjust operations to stay within the variable budget.

4. Reorganization. Operating plans and budgets can be revised to adhere to changes in the organizational structure.

The procedures that management can follow to efficiently make these adjustments using zero-base budgeting are discussed in the following sections.

REVISIONS OF PLANNING ASSUMPTIONS

In organizations that are operating in a volatile environment, or where the planning and budgeting is long drawn out, the assumptions initially provided to the managers preparing decision packages may change. Revisions are common in the manufacturing support areas, where changes in production volumes for various product lines require corresponding adjustments in the budgets for quality control, production planning and engineering, and other indirect labor activities. Capital expenditure decisions on equipment or facilities may not be made until late in the planning and budgeting cycle, or may vary with changing market projections or profitability and cash flow considerations. Changes in capital expenditures may require corresponding changes in budgets for service and support functions such as cleaning, maintenance, and utilities (in addition to the depreciation expense). Changes may also be required in research and development programs or other overhead activities (such as revising a development program because of a change in marketing requirements or expectations) although these activities are usually less sensitive to the environment than are the manufacturing service and support activities. These changes often fall into a "crack" in most planning and budgeting because management has no procedure to specifically identify which budgets need to be changed. Management may have difficulty in determining if all appropriate changes have been made because the budget numbers have not been backed up with a detailed set of planning assumptions or an analysis of each activity and its anticipated work loads.

The following procedure can be followed to revise decision packages and rankings in accordance with a revised set of planning assumptions:

1. Revise all planning assumptions and identify the changes in these revised assumptions as compared to the assumptions used by managers in preparing their current decision packages and rankings.

2. Identify the decision packages affected by these revised assumptions and modify the packages accordingly. (A central staff can identify which packages and operations are affected by the revised assumptions and can notify the affected managers of the changes. Other managers need not become involved in the revision cycle.)

3. Develop new decision packages to provide additional service and support; delete packages whose services are no longer needed.

4. Make any necessary changes in rankings, including changes in dollars and people for revised packages, new packages, or deleted packages.

This procedure allows us to concentrate on the changes required by the revised assumptions rather than revising all budget submissions, and provides management with a revised ranking that can be used to make the ultimate funding decisions.

As discussed in Chapter 1, a formalized set of planning assumptions is helpful because it provides a focal point for reviewing and revising, thereby helping to control the number of revisions in assumptions and to reduce both confusion and the continual cycling of budget inputs in rapidly changing environments. With rapidly changing assumptions we need to limit the number of revisions so that we are not constantly revising packages and rankings, and so that we can readily keep track of the assumptions used to develop any given set of packages and rankings.

The Staff and Research divisions of Texas Instruments provided the general site services and support functions (cleaning, maintenance, utilities, hiring, etc.) to the manufacturing divisions at the Dallas site. These divisions were continuously changing their production plans, revising the amount of service and support functions required and/or the amount of money they could afford to be charged for these services. We developed a series of decision packages for different levels of service (by function) for each manufacturing division so that each division could evaluate the services provided and the relative costs and benefits of each function at varying levels of service. Several divisions incorporated these packages into their own rankings so that the costs of services provided to them competed directly against the activities in their own organization (see Chapter 3 on "Subjects of Decision Packages: Service Received and Provided"). To avoid continual change, we scheduled two formalized sets of revisions in the planning assumptions: the first revision was about halfway through the planning and budgeting calendar, and the final revision was close to the end of the planning calendar. Of course, we had a final review of these packages after all budgets were approved to eliminate any mismatches created by last minute changes.

REBUDGETING

During the operating year budgets must often be revised to accommodate unanticipated needs and problems that may require budget decreases and/or increases in isolated operations or throughout the entire organization. If allowable funding levels decrease we must eliminate or reduce the level of effort on those activities least important to the organization. If allowable funding levels increase we will add to or increase the level of effort on those activities most important to the organization. The decision packages and rankings that produced the approved budget provide the perfect data base to make these changes. The following basic steps can be followed to rapidly revise budgets developed with the zero-base budgeting process:

- If the budgeted funding level must be reduced, delete those funded decision packages in order of lowest priority until the desired funding level is reached.
- If additional funds are available, add those unfunded decision packages in order of highest priority until the additional funds are exhausted.

Exhibit 6-1 illustrates the process that management might use to make a midyear budget reduction. Of course, the savings achieved by eliminating decision packages during the operating year will not usually match the costs shown on the package because some of the costs may already have been incurred or irrevocably committed. These savings may be further reduced by one-time costs of training or transferring people, or termination costs if people cannot be placed in other available positions in the organization.

The example in Exhibit 6-1 is a simplified version of the analysis required to make budget changes. The example would be realistic for an operation that did not experience any unanticipated needs or requirements but was forced to reduce expenses because of some overall division or corporate profit needs. However, most organizations do experience unanticipated needs and requirements that do require updating of

Exhibit 6-1 Midyear Budget Reduction

RANK	DECISION PACKAGE RANKING FORM: Package Name	1973 Resources		Cumulative		Worksheet: Effective Reduction Remainder of Year	
		Dollars	People	Dollars	%	Dollars	Cumulative $
126	Management Systems Education Center (1 of 2)	60	3	6980	100	27	243
127	Internal Auditing (2 of 3)	130	6	7110		63	216
128	Construction Planning (3 of 3)	25	1	7135		12	153
129	Emergency Preparation—Fire	45	1	7180		20	141
130	Manufacturing overhead control	20	2	7200	103	10	121
131	Advertising (1 of 3)	50	—	7250		20	111
132	Manufacturing overhead control (2 of 3)	33	3	7283	104	15	91
133	Personnel information system	50	2	7333		25	76
134	Product Liability Insurance	35	—	7368		35	51

↑ BUDGET REDUCTION

					APPROVED BUDGET	
135	Production Planning (3 of 3)	12	1	7380		5	16
136	Accounts Payable (2 of 3)	13	2	7393		6	11
137	Maintenance Planning (3 of 3)	12	1	7405	107	5	5
138	Operations Research	30	2	7435			
139	Cleaning (3 of 3)	145	20	7580			
140	Industrial Engineering (3 of 3)	16	1	7596			
141	Preventive Maintenance (3 of 3)	64	8	7660			
142	Purchasing (2 of 3)	15	2	7675			
143	Product Development	63	4	7738			
144	Advertising (2 of 3)	50	—	7788	111		
145	Drafting (2 of 3)	57	5	7845			
146	Product Design and Engineering (3 of 3)	30	2	7875			
147	Landscaping (2 of 3)	35	6	7910			

105

the zero-base budgeting analysis before budget changes can be made. The following steps can be taken to update the zero-base budgeting analysis:

1. Develop new decision packages to meet needs or problems not anticipated in the budget process.
2. Revise decision packages if the actual needs of the organization differ significantly from the planning assumptions used to develop the packages.
3. Modify the rankings to conform to any changes in priorities, including the new and revised decision packages.
4. Once the zero-base budgeting analysis has been updated:
• Delete those funded decision packages in order of lowest priority until the desired funding level is reached

or

• Add those unfunded decision packages in order of highest priority until the additional funds are exhausted.

This procedure may be modified somewhat to account for commitments and current staffing. If a reduction is required, management may continue to fund some lower priority packages, eliminating higher priority packages, if specific packages have already been committed by contract or start-up of a program that management does not want to recall. Also, if lower packages are already staffed and the individuals are not readily transferrable to other funded operations, management might decide to eliminate higher priority packages to avoid layoffs. However, management can avoid replacing turnover and can redirect new employees into higher priority activities.

This procedure can be done by following the steps identified, rewriting decision packages, and producing revised ranking sheets; or it can be done by top management or administrative staffs producing a work sheet to identify these changes without physically revising the packages and rankings. When the need for budget revisions occurs, there is usually no need to send back all or even most of the packages and rankings for revision. Top management and administrative staffs can follow the steps outlined, determine the basic changes indicated, and then contact the lower level managers involved in the tentative budget revisions to discuss in detail, modify, and finalize the budget revisions. This type of administrative procedure can be effective and efficient, and it avoids the confusion created if all managers who have prepared decision packages and rankings are asked to make revisions.

This administrative procedure (work sheets as opposed to physically revising the packages and rankings) was used by the Staff and Research divisions of Texas Instruments to rebudget three times during 1970 when unfavorable market conditions in the electronics industry necessitated severe budget reductions in order to keep profits at a respectable level. Excluding any delays for top management review and decision making, these budget changes could be identified and the budgets of all cost centers changed within several days. The State of Georgia also used the zero-base budgeting analysis to reduce the budget during the operating year by $57 million (about 5%), making selective reductions that varied from about 1 to 12% among the agencies.

Budget revisions based on zero-base budgeting techniques allow management to evaluate various levels of reductions or increases because of the revised rankings, to identify the consequences of various levels of budget reductions or increases through the analysis provided on each package, and to revise the operating objectives and performance expected from each activity in direct accordance with the budget changes. In addition, this analysis can be used by top management to determine the source of funds to cover cost overruns or new activities not anticipated in the budget. All too often, justifiable cost overruns or high priority new programs are funded at the expense of profits (or the taxpayer's dollar) when instead the lowest priority packages in the approved budget could be eliminated. The visibility provided by zero-base budgeting also allows top management to rob Peter to pay Paul when the budget problems of one division or operation can be offset by reducing the budgets of other divisions for the good of total corporate profits.

VARIABLE BUDGETING

Variable budgeting is a control technique to aid management in adjusting to a changing environment by providing an adjustable budget that is related to production volume. When production volume changes, the budget changes accordingly. Variable budgeting is typically associated with three categories of expense:

- Direct labor
- Direct material
- Manufacturing or operating overhead

Variable budgeting techniques do not normally encompass staff or administrative expenses, research and development, or marketing costs (except for such items as transportation and warehousing).

When a standard cost system is in use, the budget for direct labor and material is the same as the standard cost. When a standard cost system is not in use, budgeting for direct labor and material is essentially the same as setting cost standards. Labor budgets are based on time study standards and projected labor costs, and material budgets are based on engineering specifications and projected price levels. Variance analyses of actual versus standard or budgeted costs by product or product line readily identifies to management the problem areas and indicates the corrective action required.

Management has had much greater difficulty in budgeting and controlling manufacturing and operating overhead costs than it has had with direct labor and material costs. The difficulty with these overhead costs is created by several factors:

• Overhead costs are incurred in many organizational units and include a variety of dissimilar activities with different behavior characteristics.
• Activities may not be directly identifiable with a unit of product.
• Complex relationships exist between overhead activities and units of product.
• Overhead costs can lead, coincide with, or lag behind production.
• Work load volumes may bear no relationship to production activities.

These management problems in the manufacturing overhead activities are further compounded by production volume fluctuations, since management cannot readily vary its manufacturing overhead costs as rapidly as it can its direct labor and material costs, and management is faced with cost overruns if the overhead structure is maintained through periods of low production in anticipation of increased production volumes. Management is often faced with expensive time lags between reduced production volume and reduced overhead costs, with operating problems if heavy cost-cutting efforts produce unbalanced support services, or with the expensive proposition of rebuilding support functions with increased production or repairing the production problems caused by a hastily dismantled support structure.

Management has attacked some of these problems by the use of variable budgeting techniques, generally employing the type of analysis shown in Exhibit 6-2. Although individual overhead activities are not directly related to production volume, the aggregate costs of overhead functions often bear a general relationship to production volume (unit volume, direct labor costs, or other specific measures associated with

Exhibit 6-2

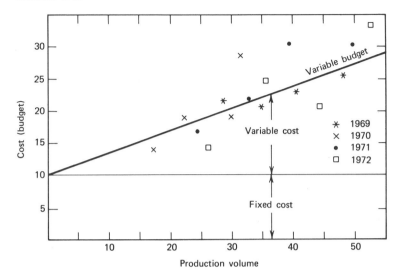

production). Initial attempts to establish the relationship between manufacturing overhead expense and production volume are usually made by historically plotting actual production volumes against overhead costs and drawing a line through these points, using eyeball or statistical techniques. This line therefore produces the variable budget by determining the allowable cost or budget at any given production volume, and can be used to develop standard overhead costs. This preliminary approach may be refined by isolating activities or costs from the aggregate of all manufacturing overhead (such as isolating utilities that may bear a relationship to machine hours), or refining the aggregate measurement of fixed and variable costs by determining the fixed and variable portions of each activity and adding the component parts to produce the total aggregate.

Although this variable budgeting technique provides management with standard costs or a budget at any production level, it does not provide management with needed answers to the following questions:

1. How much excess cost are we building into the standard or budgeted cost because of past and present inefficiencies?

2. Could we draw the variable budget line through the lowest point (best performance) rather than the average so as to set a tight standard?

3. If special production problems cause increased expenditures in

support functions (industrial, engineering, production planning, maintenance, etc.), should these expenditures be funded by allowable cost overruns or should other overhead activities be reduced?

4. How significantly can these costs be varied over the short term to help solve profit problems?

5. What actions should be taken if actual costs exceed budget or standard?

Direct labor variances indicate that management should vary the size of the work force, average hours worked per employee, and so forth, for a specific product line; direct material variances indicate that management needs to vary the inventory levels or the rate at which material is purchased. Unfortunately, variable budgeting techniques for manufacturing overhead expense are usually limited to informing management that costs are out of line and do not indicate what specific actions should be taken, how far costs can realistically be reduced, or what the impact of reduced costs would be on each activity and the manufacturing operation as a whole. The adjustment of manufacturing overhead costs is not a single event but a series of events affecting some or all of the service and support activities within the manufacturing overhead umbrella.

Zero-base budgeting complements and supplements the variable budgeting efforts for manufacturing overhead. Zero-base budgeting provides a sound basis for developing the variable budget or standard costs and identifies the specific actions necessary to correct cost variances, fund new activities or cost overruns, or increase profit margins (see the previous section on "Rebudgeting"). As mentioned in Chapter 1, zero-base budgeting does not apply to all manufacturing or operating overhead costs (such as depreciation expense or utilities), but it does apply to most other overhead costs, which are usually the most difficult to control. The quality control example in Chapter 3 is a good example of how variable budgeting and zero-base budgeting techniques work together. The cost of quality control, assuming a fixed percent of production sampled, should vary relative to production volume and thus provide us with a variable budget. However, the zero-base budgeting analysis shows that we can also vary the percentage of the product sampled and further shows the consequences involved. Therefore, management can evaluate budget changes based on changing production volume as well as change the percent of product sampled, with the relative priority of varying the percent of product sampled as opposed to the priority of other activities identified in the decision package ranking.

Zero-base budgeting also allows management to evaluate the overhead areas outside manufacturing overhead, which are usually related to long-

Exhibit 6-3

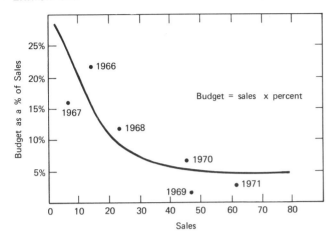

term considerations rather than short-term production volumes. A long-term variable budgeting model for nonmanufacturing overhead expense (administrative, research and development, marketing) might look like the model in Exhibit 6-3. Rather than having a linear relationship with sales (or manufacturing costs, etc.), these overhead costs at the department, division, or corporate levels might become relatively smaller in relation to sales or other costs as the organization becomes larger. Such a model might provide a long range variable budget or model against which management can evaluate current expenditure levels, but it is also subject to the same problems experienced by variable manufacturing overhead budgets and may be subject to extremely wide perturbations in the short run. To establish and modify the budget, management is again forced into a series of decisions on each of the activities comprising this overhead, and these can be made effectively and efficiently using zero-base budgeting. The variable budgeting model therefore provides a general reference to put these costs into perspective, with zero-base budgeting providing the operating tool to adjust and control each activity within the overhead structure.

REORGANIZATION

Industry and government are constantly changing their organizational structures to improve operations, solve specific operating or personnel problems, or meet the needs of the changing environment. If we establish a completely new organization or operation that has never existed before under any organizational structure, then we can develop new decision packages and rankings to produce the operating plan and budget, or we can use whatever budgeting or estimating techniques were used in the past to prepare the initial budget—implementing zero-base budgeting later, after the organization has been staffed and has developed its basic operating structure. However, most reorganizations involve changes that affect present organizations and budgets, which we must realign and rebudget to reflect the new organizational structure. This reorganization may take place during the budget process or the operating year, and often poses a serious budgeting problem when major changes occur in large organizations. To ensure an effective budget for the reorganized operations, we must (1) ensure that no activities are double-budgeted or fall in the crack with no budget, (2) identify any cost efficiencies produced by the reorganization and ensure that these cost savings are realized by incorporating the savings into the appropriate budgets, (3) and ensure that any one-time costs of re-organization are added to the appropriate budgets. These problems are especially tricky when many administrative, service, and support activities are involved.

The basic procedure to produce this realigned budget is to take the decision packages and rankings prepared under the current organizational structure, modify and/or rearrange these packages to fit the new organizational structure, and revise the budgets accordingly. If the reorganization takes place during the operating year (with the revised budget reflecting the reorganized structure for the remainder of the operating year), management can reuse the packages and rankings that established the existing budget as the basis to make any revisions. If the reorganization is identified during the planning and budgeting cycle after the preliminary packages and rankings have been prepared (possibly because of the analysis provided by zero-base budgeting), these pack-ages and rankings can then be revised to reflect the new organizational structure. If the reorganization is identified at the beginning of the plan-ning and budgeting cycle before developing the packages and rankings, the packages and rankings may be prepared reflecting the organizational changes so that no further adjustments are necessary. (This may not always be feasible because top management may not have identified in detail the changes desired, or may wish to await the zero-base-budget-ing analysis to help identify the specific changes.)

The State of Georgia went through a major reorganization during the first year that zero-base budgeting was implemented. This reorganization reduced the number of budgeted agencies by about two-thirds and included hundreds of "management improvement and cost reduction" recommendations that had budgetary impact. The basic need for reorganization was identified before the start of zero-base budgeting but the specific changes desired were not yet determined. The agencies initially prepared their packages and rankings under the existing organizational structure, and these were then used as sources of data for analysis in the reorganization study, providing many suggestions for changes and improvements. Once the reorganization structure had been determined, the packages and rankings were modified to produce a budget recommendation to the Legislature that reflected the proposed organizational structure.

The following procedures can be used to restructure decision packages and rankings to reflect organizational changes:

1. *Identify decision packages affected by the reorganization.*
- In almost all cases decision packages will be prepared below the organizational entities identified as part of the reorganization, so most packages will not have to be split among new organizational units.
- The initial pass at budgeting may be taken by sorting packages into their new organizational alignments, with the needed refinements obtained by following steps 2 or 3, below, and step 4.

2. *Finalize the budget for a currently existing organization* (the major part of the organization will remain intact, with decision packages added or deleted from step 1).

(a) For decision packages added to the organization:
- Modify these packages as required.
- Modify other packages within the organization (supervision, services, overhead, etc.) as required.
- Determine the levels of effort desired for each activity (this may be done by merging these packages into the overall ranking or making an independent judgment on each activity).

(b) For decision packages deleted from the organization:
- Remove all packages from the existing ranking.
- Modify other packages within the organization as required.
- Identify savings for reduced supervision, services, overhead, and so on, and adjust these packages accordingly.

3. *Develop a budget for a new organization* (one developed by consolidating the functions of several organizations, or an existing one that has major organizational changes that require major package revisions and invalidate the rankings prepared under the old structure).

(a) For the decision packages identified in step 1:

- Modify these packages as required, identifying cost savings, improved operations, and operating relationships with other activities.
- Delete packages whose services are no longer required.

(b) Develop packages to provide for new operations, administration, support services, and so on.

(c) Rank all packages so that the funding levels can be determined, or make independent judgments on each activity.

4. *Identify costs or cost savings created by the reorganization.*

- Incorporate one-time costs for such things as moves and rearrangements into the appropriate budget.
- Ensure that all cost savings have been incorporated into the budget.

Zero-base budgeting provides a sound basis for making the budget changes required by reorganization, with the revised packages and rankings identifying the operating objectives and performance measures for each activity in the new organizational structure.

CHAPTER 7

MANAGING THE
ZERO-BASE BUDGETING PROCESS

It has already been stated that zero-base budgeting is a basic planning and budgeting philosophy with a very flexible set of procedures that need to be adapted to fit the specific needs of each user. In addition, each user may also need to allow flexibility within his own organization to meet specific needs and problems that may vary significantly among divisions or departments. This chapter identifies the design needs and management problems that each organization will face when installing and administering zero-base budgeting. This discussion is divided into four segments:

1. Designing of implementation procedures to meet the specific needs of each organization.
2. Policy decisions that top management must make to handle common situations consistently across all units.
3. Management problems relating to the specific nature of operations and management capabilities (as distinguished from those problems associated with the zero-base budgeting process itself, as discussed in Chapter 2).
4. Should zero-base budgeting be done every year?

The use and modification of zero-base budgeting in subsequent years will depend on the effectiveness and problems experienced during the first year. This chapter is aimed primarily at those organizations initially installing zero-base budgeting, and hopefully the identification and discussion of management needs and problems will help to reduce or avoid these problems for organizations initiating this process.

DESIGNING IMPLEMENTATION PROCEDURES

Each organization must design for itself the procedures that the organization will follow to implement zero-base budgeting. This design must encompass the following subjects:

1. Where should zero-base budgeting be installed—across the entire organization, or on a trial basis in one or several departments?
2. At what organizational levels should decision packages be developed?
3. What should be the format of the decision package and ranking forms, and do these formats need to differ among organizations?
4. How should the review and ranking process proceed; to what organizational levels should the rankings be consolidated; and how should the ranking be done?
5. What planning assumptions and guidelines are required for managers to effectively prepare and rank the decision packages?
6. How should the process be administered and communicated?
7. What time requirements or calendar of events is needed to implement the process?

These questions need to be answered before the process is initiated. However, most organizations will find that they have some flexibility during the process to alter the levels at which packages are developed, the review and ranking procedures, the planning assumptions, and the time requirements. It is much more difficult, if not impossible, to initiate zero-base budgeting in an organization if this decision is made late in the budgeting process when time is not available to effectively implement the process, or to revise the original forms after managers have already completed them. Any changes during the budgeting process, especially in large organizations, are undesirable, should be avoided, and can be avoided by effectively designing the implementation procedures and anticipating the problems that will be experienced.

Questions 2, 3, and 4 were discussed in Chapters 3, 4, and 5, respectively; planning assumptions were discussed in Chapter 1, and expenditure guidelines in Chapter 5. Therefore, questions 1, 6, and 7 will be discussed in this section.

Where Should Zero-Base Budgeting Be Installed?

One of the first questions each organization must answer when initially installing zero-base budgeting is whether to install the process in one or several departments on a trial basis or to install it across the entire organization. There are several factors management should consider in making this decision:

- *Top management policy.* Top management may want to play it safe and install the process on a trial basis to see how well it works and learn how to effectively administer and use it.
- *Organization size and location.* It is more difficult to install and administer any new process in large organizations or in geographically decentralized ones.
- *Management capabilities.* If managers are accustomed to financial analysis and justification of expenditures and do not need substantial assistance in analyzing their activities, zero-base budgeting can be expanded over a larger organization because these managers will have less difficulty in analyzing their operations and developing decision packages.
- *Organizational depth of decision package development.* It becomes more difficult to administer and manage the zero-base budgeting process with increasing volumes of packages and numbers of managers participating. If decision packages are prepared at higher organizational levels, or summary packages are prepared that encompass several discrete activities, management can more readily expand the process across larger organizations. For the first year's implementation, it is common for decision packages to be developed by a central staff that summarizes the activities (including different levels of effort) of far-flung field operations, with the preparation of packages fanned out to the field operations in subsequent years.
- *Time.* The availability of adequate time to plan and administer allows effective implementation across larger organizations.
- *Format of forms.* Management may be uncertain about the format and information desired on the decision package and ranking forms, and may want to try one or several formats on a trial basis before expanding to the entire organization.

These considerations and the uncertainty in trying any new process usually causes management to try new procedures on a trial basis before jumping in feet first with the entire organization. However, there are also several problems to be considered if zero-base budgeting is installed on a trial basis only:

- Many managers are willing to try zero-base budgeting if everyone else does but will not otherwise volunteer to stick their necks out, possibly get their budgets cut, and spend time justifying current operations.

• Zero-base budgeting often produces budget reductions in current operations. Will a budget reduction hasten or hamper the expansion of the process into other operations?

• Managers can only learn the process effectively by doing it on their own operations, and unless there are some procedural changes made because of the first year's trial implementation each organization will go through the same learning curve problems regardless of the experience gained by the managers in another department or division.

These considerations do not provide a universal solution for all organizations, and—again—each organization must make its own decision.

At Texas Instruments, we installed zero-base budgeting across the Staff and Research divisions the first year, and fanned-out to all other divisions the second year. In the State of Georgia, we used the process in all 65 executive agencies the first year, despite the considerations of size, geographical location, and management capabilities that indicated that zero-base budgeting be done on a trial basis. There were three overriding considerations that caused us to implement the process across all agencies: (1) Governor Carter had committed himself to making major improvements in the effectiveness and efficiency of state government and wanted all agencies to participate if possible. (2) The agencies were given about three months longer than they had under the previous budget process to organize and install zero-base budgeting—as it turned out, the agencies took only about four months to *complete* the process, and next year the start of the process will probably be moved back to about the same time frame as the previous budgeting procedure. (3) It was anticipated that agencies would get some funding reductions in their current operations and that the other agencies would then fight the implementation of the process the second year.

Administration and Communication

The administration and communication of zero-base budgeting was very similar in Texas Instruments and the State of Georgia, with the biggest difference being a direct result of the much greater magnitude of state operations. Zero-base budgeting was administered by each divisional control department in Texas Instruments, working directly with the cost center managers in each division who prepared the decision packages. In Georgia, the Budget Bureau administered the process across the 65 agencies and assisted each agency in developing its own zero-base budgeting team, which actually administered the process within each agency. The zero-base budgeting philosophy and procedures were communicated in both organizations through a manual of instructions (see Appendix A), as well as verbal presentation and discussion of the procedures and forms with the managers who would be preparing the packages. This communication was achieved by sending manuals to those managers who would be preparing packages, and then having group meetings, ranging from several to several hundred people, for the verbal presentation and discussion of the process.

In several discussions with state budget bureaus outside Georgia, it was interesting to find that most bureaus were astounded that zero-base budgeting was administered in Georgia with only 10 analysts from the Budget Bureau. It was pointed out to these managers that zero-base budgeting is a tool for agency or division use and requires the active administration and participation of operating managers within these organizations. A large centralized administrative staff defeats this intent, and a small central staff for coordination and assistance purposes is all that is needed, with the bulk of the work done by agency or division operating managers. In Georgia, we therefore requested that each agency develop its own team, which worked in conjunction with the Budget Bureau. The size of each team varied with the size of its agency. It consisted of financial, administrative, and operating managers, and had the responsibility for effectively administering the zero-base budgeting process within each agency.

The following administrative steps may be followed for the implementation of zero-base budgeting by a small centralized staff throughout a large organization containing numerous divisions, departments, or agencies:

1. *Organization and planning.*

(a) Develop zero-base budgeting procedures, manual of instructions, forms and calendar of events for division or agency completion dates for top management review. (This development should include division or agency participation.)

(b) Establish centralized staff (or team) to implement and coordinate the process among the organizations and to provide the staff support and analysis for top management.

(c) Have each division or agency director assign an individual within his organization to be responsible for implementing the process and developing their own organizational teams.

(d) Review zero-base budgeting philosophy, procedures, and instructions with division directors and zero-base budgeting teams.

(e) Division teams determine the organizational level within their divisions where packages should be developed. (This level may be altered as the agency teams get a feel for the packages being prepared, and each manager preparing packages should feel free to subdivide his activities below the organizational level specified.) Teams also determine the levels to which the packages should be ranked. (Suggestions for the ranking procedure may be provided by central or agency teams to aid operating managers, but these managers should be given complete freedom as to how they do their rankings.)

(f) Teams develop any necessary planning or expenditure guidelines, program and policy directions, and so on, that are needed by managers preparing packages.

(g) Divisions prepare their own internal calendar for rankings, reviews, and submission dates to meet the overall calendar requirements established by top management.

2. *Implementation.*

(a) Division teams distribute the zero-base budgeting manuals and forms to managers who will be preparing decision packages.

(b) Teams conduct meetings to explain and discuss procedures and forms with managers preparing packages.

(c) Teams work with the managers preparing packages to:
• Help determine the cost for each function.
• Provide assistance in making financial analyses.
• Reevaluate level at which packages are being prepared.

(d) Throughout implementation, teams and top division management keep informed of progress and problems, sit in on lower level reviews to gain a better understanding of packages, identify problem areas in time for action to be taken, and keep lower level managers from wasting time in developing unnecessary packages.

Time Requirements or Calendar of Events

The time required to implement zero-base budgeting depends on the nature of each organization and the other six implementation subjects identified in this section. The time requirements fall into five broad categories shown below, with the approximate time ranges (in weeks) required by Texas Instruments and the State of Georgia to implement zero-base budgeting the first year indicated for each category.

Texas Instruments (time in weeks)	State of Georgia (time in weeks)	Time Required To
		1. Establish implementation procedures and communicate process to the appropriate managers.
2–4	3–6	2. Develop decision packages and make the initial ranking of these packages at the level where the packages are developed.
3–4	4–6	3. Review and rank packages at the various consolidation levels to produce a final consolidated ranking; some revisions will result from these reviews.
1–2	2–4	4. Prepare for top management review; top management review and funding decisions.
2–3	3–4	5. Revisions of packages and rankings required by top management.
8–13 (10 = average)	12–20 (15 = average)	

These time requirements indicate the range of calendar weeks allotted for each category, but do not indicate the actual time spent on the process by the managers involved. For example, managers may be given 4 weeks to develop their packages and submit them to their boss for consolidation with his other packages, but the manager who develops the packages may spend only a few man-days analyzing his operations and developing his packages during this 4-week period (and is basically finished with the zero-base budgeting process after this submission except for any participation in higher level review sessions and any required revisions). Intermediate level managers may spend only several hours or days reviewing and ranking packages, but a week or so may be allowed for the ranking at each consolidation level because managers have scheduling problems and must mesh these ranking sessions in with their other duties. The review with top management may only take several hours, with the preparation time needed depending on the type of review. For the Staff and Research divisions of Texas Instruments, with 300 decision packages, top management reviewed all packages and rankings (concentrating on the more discretionary packages) and spent almost a full day in this review.

Only a short time was needed to prepare for the top management review at Texas Instruments since the Staff and Research managers were extremely familiar with the packages by this time. In the State of Georgia, with 10,000 decision packages and 65 agencies, the packages and rankings were submitted to the Budget Bureau from 2 to 4 weeks before the Governor's review with the agencies so that this staff could analyze the material in order to present their analysis and recommendations to the Governor. Part of this staff analysis time was required so that programs that cut across agency organizational lines could be evaluated. (This is a common problem in many state organizations, although not usually in industry.) The Governor then spent from half an hour to 4 or 5 hours making a summary review with each agency, as described in Chapter 5.

These time requirements can be trimmed substantially by compressing the ranking time allotted and reducing the number of consolidation levels. Also, if the process is well managed with good planning assumptions and expenditure guidelines, the time allotted for revision after top management's initial review can be virtually eliminated. However, when implementing the process for the first time, additional time should be allowed for numerous revisions of packages at lower organizational levels, and additional time should be allowed for reviewing and ranking if the middle level managers are not familiar with the activities.

Establishing the calendar of events to implement zero-base budgeting is a two-stage process:

1. Establish the starting date for the managers to be instructed in the philosophy and procedures of zero-base budgeting and set the dates for the decision packages and rankings to be submitted for top management review.

2. Within these starting and ending dates, each organization developing one consolidated ranking must set up its own internal calendar for the ranking and reviewing sessions for each of the lower consolidation levels.

In establishing these calendars, management must make sure to allow adequate time for managers to develop decision packages. Top managers often play it safe by allowing plenty of time for their reviews, and get this time by squeezing the lowest level managers. However, if the managers preparing the packages do not have adequate time for their analyses, or to obtain assistance if needed, then the time spent by higher levels of management will be wasted because of the poor quality of the packages and the whole process will have to be recycled.

Exhibit 7-1 illustrates a typical calendar of events that might be used

Exhibit 7-1   Sample Calendar of Events

Time	Event
September 1	Issue manual of instructions; hold meeting(s) to discuss zero-base budgeting concept and procedures, expenditure and planning guidelines, and calendar of events.
September 2–24	Managers develop decision packages and make initial ranking of their packages.
September 25	Submit packages and rankings to the first consolidation level for review and ranking; revise packages as required.
September 26–October 15	Make intermediate level rankings; revise packages as required.
October 16–17	Review and rank packages at the final consolidation level.
October 25	Packages and rankings reviewed by top management; preliminary funding decisions made.
October 28	Revise planning assumptions if necessary; communicate top management instructions to those managers where changes are required.
October 29–November 9	Revise decision packages and rankings as required.
November 10	Managers at the final consolidation level review changes and rerankings to be submitted for the final top management review.
November 15	Final review of packages and rankings by top management; final decision making.
November 20	Funding decision and approved decision packages communicated throughout the organization.
December–January	Detailed costing, quarterly or monthly allocation of costs, or any other finalization steps required for internal control and management purposes.

in a medium sized division or agency, that might develop from 200 to 400 decision packages, with three or four consolidation levels required to produce the final ranking. This calendar, with the same relative time frames, may be moved into a different time frame during the year; or the time period between the final consolidated ranking and the top management review can be lengthened if administrative staffs such as that of the Georgia Budget Bureau need additional analysis and preparation time. However, small organizations or units developing one consolidated ranking may require only one month for the entire process.

In subsequent implementations, the allotted time frame may be considerably shortened, with a reduction in time of ¼ to ½ not uncommon. After the first year's implementation, each organization should be able to establish an appropriate calendar that shortens the time allotted, yet does not impose severe work load problems on any level of management.

POLICY DECISIONS

In implementing zero-base budgeting, there will be situations or needs particular to each organization for which management must make policy decisions to ensure uniform application within the organization. It can become extremely confusing if various managers handle common situations in different ways. There are several common policy decisions that most organizations must make:

- What figures should we use for the current year's cost?
- How should we handle wage and salary increases?
- How should we handle cost adjustments, lapse factors, and so on?
- How should we handle people reductions?

In addition to these policy decisions, there may be other situations that should be identified, other policy decisions that must be made, and then the entire policy communicated to the managers preparing the decision packages.

Current Year's Cost

The decision package format requires the identification of the current year's cost for every activity. However, the packages are developed to establish next year's budget and are prepared before the current year is completed. We must therefore determine what figures or what method we are going to use to calculate the current year's cost. There are three possible choices:

1. *Actual plus forecast.* The actual cost through the month or quarter at which the zero-base budgeting process begins, plus the forecast cost for the remainder of the current budget year.
2. *Budgeted cost.* The cost budgeted for each activity for the current year.
3. *Actual plus budget.* The actual cost through the month or quarter at which the zero-base budgeting process begins, plus the budgeted cost for the remainder of the current year.

The appropriate choice depends on the needs of each organization and its ability to obtain actual and forecast cost data.

We recommend that actual plus forecast cost data be used whenever possible since it reflects the truest picture of what is happening in the current year. In planning the zero-base budgeting calendar and instructions, both the time period through which actual costs will be used and the forecast period should be identified. These costs are usually available by budget unit or cost center, and these actual plus forecast costs per budget unit can then be allocated to the activities around which decision packages will be prepared. However, managers should review in detail any forecasts used to ensure that they are not inflated. If they are inflated, the costs shown for the budget year will probably be inflated, and/or the budget units will appear to have made some cost improvements for the budget year that do not really exist.

If, during the budgeting process, significant changes occur in actual versus forecast costs, or in forecast costs alone, the cost figures and decision packages may be updated on a selective basis. These variances may also be identified and analyzed without revising the packages themselves if the projected costs for the budget year are accurate. When actual and forecast costs are updated during the budgeting process, the individuals managing the process need to review any changes in forecast, make the policy decisions as to what constitutes a significant change, and determine how the changes will be handled.

The budgeted costs for each budget unit or cost center may be used, with these costs allocated to the appropriate activities for the preparation of packages. Government agencies are probably forced to use budgeted costs since they start their budgeting process at the beginning of the current budget year and therefore have little or no actual cost data for the current year. This occurs because the agency and executive budget requests must be ready for legislative review and approval about midway through the current year. Some industries may also fall into this situation, but normally they are halfway through the current year before they start to think about the coming budget cycle.

For administrative ease, budgeted costs may also be used in place of actual plus forecast costs if there are few budget variances. The budget figures may then be used, with any desired modifications to reflect the actual situation. However, management is still faced with the same policy decisions as to updating decision packages if actual costs vary significantly from budget during the zero-base budgeting process.

Actual costs through the beginning of the budget cycle, plus budgeted cost through the remainder of the current year, may be used if there is no formalized mechanism to obtain forecasts. This method provides a more accurate picture than using budgeted costs only but does not provide as accurate a picture as actual plus forecast (unless coincidence shows forecast and budget to be about equal).

Wage and Salary Increases

Every organization experiences some wage and salary increases during the budget year. Guidelines for calculating normal wage and salary increases, stipulated by contract or general policy, should be specified in the assumptions provided to the managers preparing decision packages. Most organizations prefer to incorporate these cost increases into each package. However, unusual wage and salary increases, such as major upgradings of individuals or groups, may constitute an independent decision and should therefore be displayed in a separate package or series of packages. For example, the schoolteachers in Georgia wanted a $1000 across-the-board increase in salary. A series of decision packages was prepared for this increase, with package (1 of n) showing a several hundred dollar increase, with additional increments to bring the series of packages up to the $1000 the teachers desired. These packages were ranked with all other packages, forcing management to make trade-offs among various levels of teacher raises, building new schools, and so on.

Cost Adjustments

Near the end of the budget cycle we may find that there are various cost adjustments that need to be made to the packages. If the packages show estimated costs, with the detailed cost identification by chart of accounts or line item determined after the packages have been approved, we may discover that the initial estimates need adjustment. We can make these adjustments package by package, or we can make them for each budget unit. If we find that only a few packages require adjustment, then it is better to adjust each package since it provides a better track record and avoids confusion. However, if many packages need to be adjusted, or if the detailed costing is done at the budget unit level (so that we do not know which of the packages comprising that budget unit need adjustment), it is easier to make one adjustment at the budget unit level. This can be made on a work sheet; or done by preparing a decision package for the cost adjustment (explaining the change), with the package showing a positive cost if the packages were undercosted or a negative cost if the packages were overcosted (thus we still have all our cost displayed in the same package format, which provides a good historical record).

In government, budgets often include a "lapse factor," which indicates a budget reduction resulting from an average number of vacant positions. If we budget a full year's wages, salaries, and benefits for each position, normal turnover will dictate that some of these positions will be vacant for a few weeks or months until that position is again filled. After the decision packages are approved, a package for the lapse factor can be prepared, showing a negative dollar amount—that is, the amount of the funds removed from the budget. This lapse factor package can be prepared for each budget unit if the unit contains many people and the historical turnover and replacement trend is well known. In many cases, the lapse factor must be applied against a larger organizational unit because of the turnover fluctuations at the budget unit level.

This same type of positive and negative adjustment can be made for other reasons. For example, top management may set very tight budgets at the budget unit levels but, because of business risks or the probability that some units will not be able to make their budget, may establish a "contingency fund" or "judgment" package at some top administrative level. Such a package would show a positive cost, producing a more realistic budget for the organization as a whole. However, such packages should be limited to a controlled few at top organization levels. If we let too many managers prepare these types of packages, we get inflated budgets. (Although we cannot anticipate and budget for unexpected needs, we can meet these needs and control these funds by approving budget overruns, which might be a better alternative than trying to control budgeted contingency funds setup to cover these unexpected needs.)

People Reductions

It is natural for managers to be protective of their employees. However, in developing and ranking decision packages, we cannot stress enough how important it is to develop and evaluate packages on the merit of the activity being performed. Unfortunately, it is common for managers to try to protect their people by ranking packages for current operations and staffing ahead of some higher priority new programs or activities. Assuming that we can solve the biggest part of this problem by educating the managers, as well as by making some revision in rankings where necessary, top management will nonetheless be faced fairly often with the situation that the desired funding level excludes some current operations and employees. Top management is then faced with a policy decision as to how to handle these current activities and people not funded. There are several possible alternatives:

1. Transfer the people from unfunded to funded positions where possible, crossing organizational boundaries or changing geographical locations.
2. Hope that normal turnover will solve the problem.
3. Terminate the employees (or resort to early retirement, etc.).
4. A combination of the above.

Most organizations will use some combination of the above alternatives, with termination being a last resort in industry, and often a political impossibility in government. Relying on turnover may solve the problem over a protracted period, but it still requires top management decision as to how this extension will be funded. Management can either increase the budgets to cover this extension, or keep the budget the same but temporarily eliminate or delay new programs until the current activities can be phased out. If managers physically rerank packages in order to place some lower priority current operations above the cutoff level in the total ranking, they should be extremely careful that the reason for this change is well understood by the top level managers involved, and ensure that these operations are phased out when possible and that vacancies are not filled.

Some agency managers in Georgia challenged the effectiveness of zero-base budgeting in state government because of the political impossibility of firing state employees and commented that "good employees terminate or qualify for transfers while poor employees hang on forever." However, with a 20% turnover rate experienced in many government agencies, significant reductions can take place as long as specific operations and jobs are designated to be reduced or phased out. This will still accomplish the major cost savings desired even if there are a few "hangers-on."

MANAGEMENT PROBLEMS

In Chapter 2, the general problems associated with zero-base budgeting were discussed. However, there are also additional problems associated with the implementation of zero-base budgeting or any other planning and budgeting procedure that are specific to the nature of operations along with management capabilities and attitudes in every organization. These particular problems also impact the severity of the problems discussed in Chapter 2, directly influence the ease in which each organization adopts zero-base budgeting, and determine quality of the results obtained. Perhaps the best illustration of the types of management problems that each organization can face is the following critique on the first year's implementation of zero-base budgeting in Georgia. This critique was chosen because it illustrates a wide range of problems experienced by an extremely large organization. However, many of these same problems will be experienced during the initial implementation of zero-base budgeting in either industry or government, and the illustration should be relevant to any readers interested in the implementation of the process.

Critique

It is a good management practice to make a critique of any major system or process upon completion, to identify the problems experienced, determine if the process should be repeated, and make appropriate changes before the process is repeated. The Georgia critique was aimed at identifying the problems encountered throughout the state agencies and does not attempt to identify the many benefits. Also, all the problems identified in the critique were not experienced in each agency, although most were experienced in some degree in the major agencies (budgets in excess of $100 million). The critique is out of proportion by intent, and if any agency had experienced all the problems identified in any intensity, the process could not have survived or produced meaningful results. This critique therefore plays the role of the Devil's Advocate, and was developed to identify problems that could be avoided in the future. It was not meant as a criticism of the managers throughout the State of Georgia who did a most creditable job for their initial zero-base budgeting effort.

The following critique was written after many detailed discussions with managers at all organization levels of the medium and large state agencies, and has been modified only slightly for clarification purposes, with a few references to other chapters of this book added.

ZERO-BASE BUDGETING CRITIQUE
STATE OF GEORGIA
SEPTEMBER 21, 1971

I. *Purpose of Critique*
   The purpose of this critique was to analyze (1) the impact and effectiveness of zero-base budgeting in the preparation of the FY 1973 executive budget recommendation; (2) the problems encountered; (3) the changes desired to improve the process and the results obtained; and (4) the question of whether this process should be continued.

II. *General Observations*
   1. The consensus is that zero-base budgeting can be effective and should be continued next year.
   2. The quality of the decision packages and analysis is generally poor to mediocre (with several notable exceptions); however, these results are better than anticipated. The zero-base budgeting process significantly reduced (by about 50%) the amount of additional funds requested by the agencies, but major shifts (reductions) from current programs to high priority new programs did not take place, although there were some significant internal shifts within departments. In addition, the opportunities for reducing costs and improving effectiveness were not adequately identified and evaluated. This was to be expected, and quality improvements will come naturally as agency managers continue to use this type of analysis. [*Author's note:* My very critical observation of poor to mediocre quality of the analysis was based on Texas Instruments standards, which will probably never be achieved across a large government organization. However, the analysis was significantly better than any done previously and, after all, Rome was not built in a day!]
   3. Most of the severe problems encountered this year can be avoided next year because of this year's learning experience

as well as a few minor changes in the process. Also, the agencies should then be able to channel their efforts into improving the quality and depth of analysis.

4. Some agency managers were negative about zero-base budgeting when they did not get the funds they desired.

5. This critique should be continued by working with each agency to identify those activities and operations that need substantial analysis and improvement so that the agencies can direct their efforts toward improving these areas before starting zero-base budgeting next year.

III. *Implementation Problems*

A. General

1. There is little incentive in government to be cost effective, and most cost savings were made by agency directors or the Budget Bureau by eliminating packages rather than by improving the effectiveness of the operation.

2. Some managers thought this would be a one-year exercise, with no budget decisions made from the packages, and package quality reflected this attitude.

3. Many managers developed their packages and rankings to protect their people.

4. The changes in the budget process every year confuse agency managers, put them at the bottom of the learning curve, force revisions in internal planning and control procedures, and reduce agency commitment to any given procedure.

5. Large agencies and the Budget Bureau had mechanical problems of handling and analyzing the large volume of decision packages. (Next year more packages will be developed, since managers will do a more detailed analysis and will expand the process deeper into their field operations.)

B. Planning: There is a general lack of planning (including expenditure guidelines) across state government. Therefore, some of the effort that went into zero-base budgeting was wasted because some basic policy decisions had not been made before developing the packages and rankings.

1. Policy decisions made at the Governor's review should have been made before developing decision packages.

2. Many decision packages were prepared that had no chance of being funded.

3. The dollar increments between the various levels of effort identified for many activities were too large. These packages were revised if time permitted, but in many cases the packages were discarded and arbitrary decisions were made to

determine the budget level. For example, an activity might have three levels of effort: 80, 105, and 130% of the current budget level. The 80% level might have been unrealistically low, with a 90% level being a realistic funding expectation, and the 130% level being unrealistically high, with 110% being a realistic level. (This is a common problem regardless of planning or expenditure guidelines, but it can become a major problem without guidelines, as it was this year in some agencies.)

4. The 80 and 115% expenditure guidelines were misunderstood by many agencies, which required that each activity have a minimum level of 80% or less, and often had one of the packages bring the level of effort to 115% (see Chapter 5 for a detailed discussion of guidelines and a further explanation of this problem).

C. Decision Package Formulation

1. Managers spend a great deal of time deciding the activities around which decision packages should be developed. This initial determination, with the many false starts and revisions, took about one month. This should not be a problem next year since agencies can determine before the start of the process exactly where they want packages developed—based on this year's experience.

2. Cost information was poor in many cases for several reasons:
   - Budget units encompass too many discrete activities, which makes cost allocation difficult and time consuming.
   - Many managers who prepared packages do not ever see budgets or actual costs.
   - Not enough detailed cost information was shown on the packages to evaluate the estimates, nor to evaluate line items such as travel or equipment purchases—which can be modified even if the package is approved.

3. Quantitative information was not identified and/or available, and it will probably take several years to develop adequate measures and data.

4. Alternative ways of performing each function were not adequately identified or examined; many managers did not seem to consider seriously any type of organizational changes.

5. Projections are probably not needed on the form since less than 1% of the packages actually commit the state to increases in future years that exceed 10% (which was the guideline for identifying projections). These few packages

that have projections can be readily anticipated and identified and reasonable projections could still be made if this section were not on the form.

6. There was no uniformity of approach in developing decision packages for similar operations or institutions within each agency, much less among agencies.

D. Ranking

1. Agencies with large numbers of packages (exceeding 250–300) had difficulties in producing a single agency ranking. This problem was created primarily by sheer volume, but was compounded by a lack of detailed knowledge and understanding of the activities by middle and top level agency managers, and the lack of an effective ranking procedure.

2. The fragmentation of activities into detailed functions and levels of effort made it difficult for top level managers not intimately familiar with each program to understand each package and relate its importance to the program as a whole.

3. The final agency rankings were not evaluated or measured against any goals or objectives (since there was no planning) to evaluate the impact of various levels of funding, and some of the funding recommendations seemed to be a package-by-package accumulation of costs without framework or direction.

E. Governor's Review and Budget Bureau Management

1. Some agency directors had the impression that their rankings and priorities were sacred and were extremely unhappy about the changes recommended by the Budget Bureau.

2. Many agencies were not given enough lead time before the Governor's review to analyze and understand the Budget Bureau's questions and recommendations.

3. Packages and rankings were not discussed at all in some reviews (where the Governor concentrated on policy decisions and summary analyses prepared by the Budget Bureau—which based its analyses on the packages and rankings), and a few agencies had the feeling that zero-base budgeting was not really used.

4. The computer system had many start-up and maintenance problems that required a great deal of time from the Budget Bureau analysts. These problems occurred because of the last minute haste in which the system was designed and programmed, and will be corrected before the beginning of zero-base budgeting next year. (See Chapter 9 on "Computer Applications".)

IV. *Recommendations for FY 1974*

A. General

1. The state needs to outline a program for a comprehensive planning, budgeting, and control (detail budgeting, accounting, quarterly allotment, performance auditing, etc.) system. Such a total system would improve the effectiveness of each of the parts. There are current efforts in each area that need to be coordinated and planned if they are to be effective, and this planning problem is compounded since several efforts are not in the same stage of development or implementation. (See Chapter 10.)

2. The planning and zero-base budgeting procedures need to be firmly established and maintained for the remainder of the Governor's administration. Only minor modifications to the FY 1973 format and forms are needed, so that if the agencies know that the zero-base budgeting process will be continued with only minor modifications in format, they can make their plans accordingly. By the time the next governor is elected, agencies should produce a good product with reasonable efficiency, with the process standing a good chance of being continued in following administrations.

3. Programs and budget units need to be redefined in many agencies.

4. The agencies and the Budget Bureau need a compatible computer system to handle the volume of data and analyses. This system must meet internal agency needs, with the agency program feeding the Budget Bureau system. This system should also be compatible with the total planning, budgeting, and control concept. (See Chapter 9.)

B. Planning

1. There needs to be formal planning before zero-base budgeting to set basic priorities and policy decisions and provide agencies with an anticipated funding range.

2. The anticipated funding range should reflect the established priorities, have a 5 to 10% range, yet neither guarantee any agency the lower limit of the range if it cannot be justified by the decision packages nor limit the agencies from requesting an amount in excess of the upper limit of the range.

3. This planning process needs to be kept simple so that we do not develop a full PPB system, which is being abandoned by most states. (See Chapter 8.)

4. The agencies should be allowed to present their program objectives to the Governor, using discussions and reviews

rather than long text presentation as much as possible. The Governor can then establish his priorities, policy decisions, and anticipated funding ranges. We must then ensure that the agencies establish internal planning policy and guidelines for the managers who will be preparing and ranking decision packages.

C. Decision Packages

1. Packages should be formatted to include detail cost information: personal services (salaries, benefits) plus operating expenses by account (19 accounts). This information can be computerized to produce the detailed budgets for the agencies as well as the Budget Bureau, with the exception of the detail for personal services that can be provided to a large degree from computer printouts of the merit system.

2. More uniformity in package preparation, measures of effectiveness, and so on, can be achieved through Budget Bureau coordination and internal agency planning and management.

D. Ranking

1. The organizational level within each agency to which the rankings are consolidated needs to vary by agency, depending primarily on volume of packages. The volume problem experienced this year can be readily solved by stopping the consolidation of rankings at a manageable level, such as program or department. Agency managers can then spend their time reviewing these rankings, can identify their priorities among departments or programs, and can establish the cutoff levels for each ranking for several predetermined levels of agency funding (corresponding to guidelines, goal expenditure level, etc.). This process will take about half as much time as physically merging all packages yet will not force the Governor to make trade-offs among 350 separate rankings, since each agency will have made these trade-off analyses and recommendations for the Governor's review. The final funding level can then be established, at one of the predetermined levels or some different funding level, with any desired modifications in packages and rankings.

2. More emphasis needs to be given to evaluating the impact that various funding levels have on program goals and objectives.

E. Governor's Review and Budget Bureau Management

1. The procedures to be followed in preparing the FY 1974 budget need to be established before January 1972 and com-

municated to the agencies so that they can prepare internally and develop the necessary planning and computer aids.

2. The Governor's review time can be shortened because of the planning process and the greatly improved quality of decision packages and rankings anticipated. A formal second review for all agencies probably will not be needed.

3. If the detail costing is shown on each package, the time required for this final step can be greatly shortened.

V. *Conclusion*

In summary, we believe that the pain and anxieties experienced this year can be greatly reduced in future years with the continuance of zero-base budgeting integrated with an effective planning process; and that great improvement in quality can reasonably be expected through the natural learning process and the improvements in agency and Budget Bureau management and analysis that will come with experience.

(End of Critique)

Before you get discouraged and decide that no process, however beneficial, is worth these problems, remember that most of these problems are inherent in the organization itself. If an organization has such internal management shortcomings, the zero-base budgeting process will rapidly surface them and provide a mechanism for solution. These organizations also have a great need for an effective management process, and zero-base budgeting can have a significant impact on and achieve considerable improvement in efficiency and effectiveness, although the experience may be somewhat traumatic in the beginning. Small organizations, or well managed large organizations, can achieve excellent results the first year and can avoid most of the problems identified.

The organization that would have the greatest problem in implementing zero-base budgeting is the one that has the greatest need for zero-base budgeting.

SHOULD ZERO-BASE BUDGETING BE DONE EVERY YEAR?

This question is a common topic of discussion for which there is no simple yes or no answer. During the critique of the first year's implementation of zero-base budgeting, each organization will determine whether it wants to continue the process the following year (with modifications). To date, in industry and government, the organizations have wanted to continue the process the second year for three reasons: (1) the analysis and results of the first year's effort needed improvement; (2) managers had not really learned the process and the type of analysis required was not an ingrained way of thinking; and (3) many departments wanted to expand the process deeper into their operations, especially field operations.

However, once these quality and learning problems were overcome or substantially reduced through a repeat of the process the second year, managers were again uncertain as to the need of repeating the process every year. The following questions and comments have been raised during discussions with department managers, and illustrate legitimate concerns supporting both sides of the question as to whether zero-base budgeting should or should not be done every year:

1. Arguments against yearly repetition.
- The major benefit is achieved the first year by taking a look at all activities, so why do it again?
- We will just get the same packages every year.
- Programs do not change that much so we do not need yearly reviews.
- The budget process is not the only way programs are reviewed, so programs get reviewed yearly even if we do not repeat zero-base budgeting.
- Is the extra effort really worth the added benefit every year, or would repeating this process every several years gain us almost the same benefits?
2. Concerns about not repeating the process every year.
- How will we budget in those years that we do not use zero-base budgeting?
- How will we handle changing work loads, requested increases, new programs, or program changes?
- How will we fund increases and new programs? Can we reduce any current programs to fund these increases if we have not repeated the zero-base budgeting analysis?
- Should not each manager be required to review his activities each year as a matter of standard practice, and then have the opportunity to review his operations and effectiveness with top management?
- Managers will fall back into their old patterns of looking only at the increases desired and will not continue to evaluate in detail their effectiveness and efficiency.

3. Alternative suggestions.

- Repeat the process every 2 to 3 years.
- Rotate the activities or organizations that use zero-base budgeting each year, so that some organizations are doing the process every year.
- Repeat the process only for those programs with major changes and problems so that management can concentrate on these areas.
- Repeat the process with changes of management or government administrations so that these new managers can completely review all activities, programs, and priorities.
- Use some combinations of the above recommendations.

These observations and comments all have some merit even though some are contradictory. The issue really boils down to the question, "Is the additional effort of repeating the zero-base budgeting process every year worth the effort?" Each organization must answer this question for itself.

It is clearly acceptable to repeat the process every 2 to 3 years if an organization makes its major funding allocations for such a time frame, such as a biennium budget, with these multiyear costs shown on each decision package. However, if annual budgets are used, the following two criteria should be met before zero-base budgeting should be discontinued as a standard practice every year:

1. Management must be satisfied that the operations are effective and efficient.

2. The work environment must be reasonably stable, without major changes in work loads, problems, needs, and so on.

If these conditions are met, zero-base budgeting need not be continued every year.

If the formal zero-base budgeting process is not repeated every year, the following procedures can be used to establish the budget:

- Decision packages from earlier years can be reviewed, with changes made on an exception basis, and built-in cost increases, such as wages and salaries, can be estimated for each cost center or budget unit.
- Decision packages can be developed for new activities and programs and packages can be developed for increased levels of effort for existing activities.
- Zero-base budgeting can be repeated in a few selected departments

or programs to handle special problems and modifications, or it can be repeated for those activities undergoing substantial change.

• Management can then establish its priorities and funding levels by reviewing the prior year's packages and rankings (with any modifications) and the newly developed packages. This can be physically done by merging the new packages into the prior year's ranking or it can be done by ranking the new packages, with management then comparing the new ranking and the prior year's ranking to establish the funding levels on both rankings.

This procedure would still allow new programs to be funded by reductions in current activities since we can evaluate new packages against last year's packages and rankings. We need not fall into the trap of looking only at the increases desired, and management could still be satisfied that all resources had been reviewed and were effectively allocated.

At Texas Instruments, the possibility of not repeating zero-base budgeting every year was not contemplated, primarily because change was the rule rather than the exception. So even if we were satisfied with the effectiveness of all operations, we failed the criterion of environmental stability, and therefore repeated the process every year. However, the past year's packages and analyses should be used as a building block to develop new packages, even if these new packages are almost identical to the past year's analysis. Why waste the time and effort spent then? However, most managers have some changes they want to make—such as changes in work procedures, cost updates, evaluation of quantitative package measures, replacement of equipment, or increased funds to cover inflation. For those whose operations are reasonably efficient and static, updating the past year's analysis and decision packages is quick and simple, does not impose a burden on the organization in time and effort, offers lower management an opportunity to review operations and effectiveness with top management, and allows top management to update understanding and analysis on all operations.

In conclusion, we recommend that zero-base budgeting be done every year until the mechanics of the procedure and type of analysis required become ingrained into the thought process of managers throughout the organization, which may take two or more successive budget years. After this has been done, each organization should continually evaluate the cost versus benefit of continuing the process every year—and there is no universal right answer as to whether zero-base budgeting should be done every year in every organization.

CHAPTER 8

ZERO-BASE BUDGETING AND PPB

The Planning-Programming-Budgeting (PPB) System is the primary planning and budgeting system used in federal government, and has also been adopted by many state and local governments. PPB was initiated in the Department of Defense under Robert McNamara in 1961, and was extended to all other federal agencies in 1965 by presidential directive. PPB was designed to provide a systematic process to identify trade-offs among programs aimed at similar objectives, to analyze the performance and impact of programs, and to connect these objectives with the current year's budget. PPB is aimed primarily at macroeconomic analyses of broad policy decisions and desired output rather than the nuts and bolts of detailed planning and implementation, and therefore relates most directly to long range planning in industry.

Unfortunately, PPB has fallen short of expectations in the federal government and has generally failed as a "system" in state and local governments (with state and local governments usually adopting only certain aspects of the system as defined in the Department of Defense). The problems with PPB stem from two sources:

1. Implementation problems in PPB—the way the system is defined.
2. Critical gaps in the system.

This chapter explores the critical gaps in PPB, shows how zero-base budgeting can be used to fill these gaps, and shows how zero-base budgeting can be used to reinforce PPB or to act as the primary operating and decision making tool where a full-fledged PPB system is not meaningful. This chapter is not intended as an attack on PPB, but is meant to be a constructive discussion of how zero-base budgeting can improve PPB, and vice versa.

The remainder of this chapter is divided into the following sections:

140

ŧ

- PPB: purpose, procedures, implementation problems, and accomplishments
- Critical gaps in PPB
- Zero-base budgeting as it fills the critical gaps and reinforces PPB
- Zero-base budgeting and government planning and budgeting

The description of purpose, character, implementation problems, and accomplishments of PPB has been kept to a minimum since there are numerous governmental and professional publications on the subject. The many recent improvements and innovations made in program analysis and other elements of the basic PPB structure, at all levels of government, by people such as Graeme M. Taylor of Management Analysis Center, are not discussed. These improvements strengthen the planning framework, often utilize some zero-base budgeting concepts, and go hand-in-hand with zero-base budgeting. In identifying the problems of PPB, we have limited the discussion to the problems experienced in implementing the system the way it was designed and constituted, with the section on critical gaps in PPB discussing a separate set of problems created by what the system does not cover. To avoid adding more controversy to an already controversial subject, the identification of implementation problems has been paraphrased from official governmental sources, and noted accordingly. The discussion on critical gaps in PPB and the role zero-base budgeting can play in filling those gaps and reinforcing PPB reflects my own opinions.

PPB

Purpose

PPB was initiated in the Department of Defense under Robert McNamara in 1961. Before 1961, DOD planning was done by the Joint Chiefs of Staff, with plans in terms of military forces and weapons systems projected for a 5 to 10 year period. The planning and priorities of these forces and weapons systems were left to each service (Army, Navy, Air Force), which led to duplication and imbalance. Budgeting was done on a "budget ceiling basis," with the President specifying the general level of defense expenditures and the Secretary of Defense allocating the total among the services. This procedure did not focus on long range impacts or consequences of the decisions reached, nor concentrate on performance or effectiveness, and the budget was controlled by appropriation account.

PPB was developed to provide a rational and systematic approach to identify and evaluate the costs and consequences of strategic objectives (*Planning*), translate the strategic objectives into time-phased men and material needs in each organization (*Programming*), and translate time-phased men and material needs into financial requirements (*Budgeting*). PPB was designed to encourage analysis of major policy issues and to provide a mechanism to identify the trade-offs among programs aimed at similar objectives. In President Johnson's 1965 directive ordering all federal agencies to adopt PPB techniques, five reasons were stated for the adoption:

1. To identify national goals with greater precision and determine the priority among goals.

2. To develop and analyze alternative means of achieving the goals.

3. To project long-term systems costs and relate them to the benefits of each program.

4. To specify plans for several years ahead that will achieve the stated objectives.

5. To strengthen control over programs and budgets through improved measurement and analysis of program performance in relation to cost.

These goals and programs were defined by strategic objective for the Department of Defense as a whole, with coordinated programs and subprograms developed for each of the three services to achieve the overall objectives. This intraservice planning was aimed at improving effectiveness and eliminating the duplication and imbalances.

Procedures

The procedures of PPB described in this section relate to the system as applied in the Department of Defense. Other federal agencies and state and local governments that have adopted PPB have made some modifications to the process, or have adopted only certain components of it. In the Department of Defense, there are five components of PPB:

1. Program structures
2. Issue letters
3. Special analytic studies
4. Program memoranda
5. Program and financial plans

Program structures are a grouping of activities within an agency (or among agencies) that are oriented toward a strategic objective. The purpose of the program structure is to provide a better framework for the analysis of all activities and costs relevant to a given problem, to identify differences and similarities of operations in different organizations servicing the same program or problem, and to identify trade-offs and gaps in the services provided. The basic unit of the program structure is the program element, which usually corresponds to an organizational unit within each agency to facilitate management control. Thus every organization is contained in some program element, and both agency and program totals can be obtained by adding the elements contained within the agency or program structure, regardless of the number of programs within each agency or the number of different agencies participating in the same program. This crosswalk between program and agency organizational structure is shown in Exhibit 8-1.

Exhibit 8-1   Agency Organization and Program Structures

Agency organization:

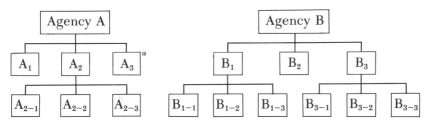

Program structure:

	Program X	Program Y	Program Z
	A_1	A_3	A_{2-3}
	A_{2-1}	B_2	B_{1-1}
	A_{2-2}	B_{3-1}	B_{1-2}
		B_{3-2}	B_{1-3}
		B_{3-3}	

[a] Program elements: program elements may be defined at different organizational levels within each agency, depending on the size and nature of operations.

In the Department of Defense, for example, there are 10 major programs:

1. Strategic forces
2. General purpose forces
3. Intelligence and communications
4. Airlift and sealift

5. Guard and reserve forces
6. Research and development
7. Central supply and maintenance
8. Training, medical, and other general personnel activities
9. Administration and associated activities
10. Support to other nations

Each of these 10 major programs is composed of numerous elements, which are organizational units within each of the three services. Imposed between the program and the element are program subtotals called program categories, which group similar elements (producing a program structure similar to an organization chart). Three are over 100 program elements defined in the Department of Defense, which would put the cost of the average element at around $75 million. Of course, the size and nature of programs and program elements can vary significantly among and within agencies, with the size of elements ranging from the hundreds of thousands to the hundreds of millions of dollars.

Issue letters identify the major policy issues that need to be evaluated during the planning and budgeting cycle. Issue letters are developed through consultations between each agency and the Budget Bureau in the federal government, with formal letters issued by the Budget Director early in the cycle. Issue letters are used to focus limited analytic resources on the most important problems, to reach early agreement about the nature of the problems, and to identify the range of alternatives to be evaluated by each agency. This step is followed by the special analytic studies that concentrate on the issues identified, which are in turn followed by the program memoranda that summarize the agency decisions and analyses on the issues identified.

Special analytic studies include any analyses of a particular problem or issue. Such studies can be aimed at issues to be evaluated and decided upon during either the current or some future planning and budgeting cycle and can include mathematical models, economic studies, data collection, development of new techniques, and so forth. These studies concerning current issues should provide the connecting link between the issue letters that identify the problem and the program memoranda that recommend a solution.

Program memoranda summarize agency decisions on the major issues identified in each program category. These memoranda relate to the issue analysis, identify the alternatives considered, and state the assumptions made in the analysis. This formalized step helps ensure that issues are decided on some logical rationale rather than being determined by accident or precedent, identifies similar issues among agencies, and serves as a means of establishing and communicating policy directives within each agency.

Program and financial plans display historical and projected funds (as well as program output measures where available) for each program category committed by previous decisions and current requests. These plans display the actual data for the two preceding fiscal years, and the projection of funds committed for the next 5 years. The plans attempt to bridge the gap between long-term strategic objectives and plans and the current year's budget allocation, to identify that portion of future budgets that are "committed" by current and past decisions, and to identify the future consequences of current decisions.

These five components of PPB have not been applied identically or uniformly throughout federal, state, and local governments. Many agencies have adopted or emphasized only certain aspects of the system, concentrating on the program structure, multiyear projections, or analysis aspects while ignoring the other components of PPB. This brief discussion on the character of PPB merely indicates the basic philosophy and procedures of the system. However, PPB is still evolving, with the various agencies beginning to modify and adapt the system (or parts of it) to more closely fit their needs and capabilities.

Implementation Problems

PPB has not lived up to its initial billing and the expectation that it would create a management revolution in government—a statement that is made by even the strongest advocates of the system. PPB has not produced visible changes in the decision making process and budgets produced, and has produced widespread dissatisfaction in government —as evidenced by the multitude of opposition statements and criticisms expressed in professional publications as well as in testimony to the Congressional Subcommittee on Economy in Government.*

Some critics talk about the difficulty of program evaluation and the need for policy analysis that delves into questions such as the purpose of government, the means of measuring program impact on the marginal utility of the public good, or the distribution of wealth and the rights to that wealth. These may be legitimate academic criticisms and concerns, but they are often meaningless to agency managers who operate

---

* Joint Economic Committee, U.S. Congress, *The Analysis and Evaluation of Public Expenditures: The PPB System*, 91st Congress, 1st Session (May, 1969), vols. 1–3.

in a world where their programs are justified by precedent, political considerations, and subjective judgment—not by economic considerations. Some of the attack is based on the decisions made while using PPB, such as the controversial decisions on the intraservice TFX (F-111) aircraft, B-70 bomber, or nuclear-powered aircraft carriers; or the criticism leveled at the PPB because it has not produced good budget allocations according to some given individual's opinion. These charges can be leveled against the best or worst systems. However, such comments reflect negatively on the decision makers themselves rather than on the system—as long as the system identified and evaluated the alternatives—or they reflect negatively on the individuals performing the analyses—if their assumptions and analyses did not prove to be valid.

Apart from these general criticisms, which can be leveled at any decision making process in government, let us briefly summarize the major problems in implementing PPB in government. And here, as stated earlier, to avoid further controversy let us paraphrase the observations of Jack W. Carlson (Assistant Director of Program Evaluation of the U.S. Bureau of the Budget) in his paper submitted to the Subcommittee on Economy in Government.* Although these comments are directed at problems experienced in the federal government, state and local governments appear to have experienced most of the same problems. Mr. Carlson lists two types of problems in implementing PPB in federal government: (1) general problems in government decision making, and (2) specific problems in the formal PPB structure:

1. General problems in government decision making in a large and highly complex organization, with many levels of authority, in an intense political environment.
- Demand for services exceeds revenue sources, with most requests having some merit.
- Legal and moral commitments made by past decisions greatly limit the remaining portion of the budget that can be exercised.
- Evaluation and coordination of programs is difficult, with evaluation not always tied into the decision making process.
- Implementing new ideas (such as PPB) is difficult.
- Ineffective or overcostly programs may continue indefinitely because of moral or political claims, with the resulting need for a method

---

* Jack W. Carlson, "The Status and Next Steps for Planning, Programming and Budgeting," in Joint Economic Committee, U.S. Congress, *The Analysis and Evaluation of Public Expenditures: The PPB System,* 91st Congress, 1st Session (May, 1969), pp. 613–634.

to identify these programs and develop less costly or more effective solutions.

• Planning methods have not met these difficulties, and therefore better linkage is required between long range plans and resources available.

• Predetermined funding levels are normally not changed even if work load or performance standards are not met.

2. Specific problems in the formal PPB structure.

• PPB has developed into a parallel path for decision making and budgeting and is in some cases a competitive method to the traditional channels of budgeting and appropriation. These dual systems reduce the effectiveness of both methods because of limited time and analytic resources.

• Program structures have not been uniform in quality or usefulness, have not proved to be a central focus for decision making, and have not generated the anticipated in-depth reevaluation of program content and alternatives.

• Issue letters have not always been developed early enough in the planning cycle to be effective, issues have not always been well defined, and only a fraction of the issues were analyzed (50% in 1969).

• Program memoranda have been descriptive and nonanalytic accounts of existing and proposed programs, containing pleas for approval of the full request. Most memoranda have not identified major alternatives, not concentrated on policy issues, and not outlined a multiyear program to achieve objectives.

• Special analytic studies have been constrained because of the many layers of government, each with the capability of inhibiting change. Some agencies have concentrated on minor issues, and many studies do not cover broad program problems if they are related to several agencies.

• Program and financial plans have included lengthy wish lists that bore no relationship to realistic funds available, and the subsequent requirement that projections include only those funds "committed" by past and present decisions has produced inconsistent results because of the variable interpretations of what constitutes a commitment.

The general problems experienced in implementing PPB reflect some of the same type of general problems encountered in installing zero-base budgeting in Georgia (see Chapter 7), and seem to reflect the nature of the animal—government. Another problem usually identified, which often receives the major blame for poor results of PPB, is the lack of a well trained staff to install and administer the system. This problem usually occurs because PPB is implemented by a centralized staff, one in each agency in federal government, and one in most state and local governments. With the budget analysts proceeding along their parallel paths of budgeting as usual, this existing manpower resource must be augmented to install PPB.

These problems do not spell the demise of PPB in government. Mr. Carlson concludes that the executive branch in federal government still pursues the objective of PPB, while also making changes to minimize the problems and improve the decision making process. State and local governments will probably continue to adopt those portions of PPBS that meet their needs and capabilities.

In summarizing the implementation problems of PPB (limiting these comments to PPB as it is defined), we can make the same basic conclusion we made in Chapter 7 about the implementation problems of zero-base budgeting in state government: The organization that would have the greatest problem in implementing [the system] is the one that has the greatest need for [the system].

Accomplishments

The negative reaction to PPB stems in part from the high hopes and expectations when it was initially implemented. However, to put PPB into proper perspective, it is only fair to compare the improvements or accomplishments that the system has produced over the pre-PPB days. Referring again to Jack W. Carlson's paper submitted to the Subcommittee on Economy in Government, Mr. Carlson identifies nine areas of improvement associated with PPB:

1. *Definition of objectives.* Better understanding of problems and alternatives and some reappraisal of functions and objectives.
2. *Information.* Improved information on program inputs and outputs as related to objectives.
3. *Use of analysis in decision making.* Although analysis and decision making have not always been connected, agencies have substantially increased useful analysis.
4. *Evaluation of programs.* Increased efforts to measure program accomplishments and evaluate program concepts.
5. *Management efficiency.* Some attempts to identify actual expenditures and measure them against predetermined program plans.
6. *Involvement of officials in the budget process.* Increased awareness

by top agency officials that for policy decisions to be meaningful they must be translated into a budget.

7. *Recognition of the legitimacy and necessity of analytic argument.* Increased recognition that analysis does have a place in influencing decisions, along with political and subjective factors.

8. *Comparisons of related programs in several agencies.* Identification of program purpose and context makes it easier for analysts to identify and compare related programs in different organizations.

9. *State and local interest.* Federal assistance has aided state and local governments in developing their own PPB systems, which is important in itself and will eventually affect those federal programs that depend on effective state and local participation.

Although these accomplishments are highly qualified, they do point to improvements over the pre-PPB situation.

CRITICAL GAPS IN PPB

One major reason that PPB has not been effective and has not provided a major operating and decision making tool lies in the design of the system itself. PPB is basically a macroeconomic, centralized, top-down policy and long range planning tool. This orientation leaves five critical gaps in a system designed as the decision making tool for planning and budgeting in government:

1. PPB focuses on what will be done, not how to do it.
2. Budgeting as defined by PPB is a cost calculation based on the decisions made in the planning and programming steps (or long range planning phase), whereas there are in reality many policy decisions and alternatives to be evaluated during the actual budget preparation.
3. PPB does not provide an operating tool for the line managers who implement the policy and program decisions.
4. PPB does not provide a mechanism to evaluate the impact of various funding levels on each program and program element, or establish priorities among the programs and varying levels of program effort.
5. PPB focuses primarily on new programs or major increases in ongoing programs and does not force the continual evaluation of ongoing program activities and operations.

PPBS has no formal methodology to transform policies and objectives into an efficient operating plan and budget. Recognizing the real world in which government managers operate, where economic considerations do not always prevail in determining program structure and content, we can see that any planning and budgeting system must emphasize the need for carrying out each program at minimum cost.

PPB focuses on the effect that a group of activities has in achieving certain objectives rather than the efficiency in which each activity is carried out. Proponents of PPB will argue that the limited analytic resources should be spent on evaluating program effectiveness rather than in concentrating on operational efficiency. Who wants an Edsel—or a program that cannot achieve its objectives even if it is efficiently implemented? However, this is a somewhat hollow argument. With severely limited resources, the inefficient use of any resources limits the amount of effort and funds available and will in turn limit the effectiveness of programs that need these additional resources to be effective. Therefore the macroeconomic planning and policy making process must be effectively linked with a microeconomic planning and budgeting technique. The hypothesis of this book, of course, is that zero-base budgeting provides this microeconomic link to fill the gaps in PPB.

Budgeting in the PPB system is a cost calculation based on the decisions made in the planning and program evaluation stages. The lowest unit evaluated in the PPB structure is the program element, which can encompass extremely large and complex operations in many agencies. Once the major policy decisions have been made for these elements, there are many detailed policy decisions to be made and alternatives to be evaluated in determining the final budget. If we are evaluating mental health, for example, and make the policy decisions that the emphasis is going to be changed from institutional care to community health programs, some of the following decisions must be made during the detail planning and budgeting phase:

- Should community health centers be large and centrally located, or should they be small and located in each neighborhood, or can these decisions vary by location? How many centers should we add each year and where should they be located?
- How should we staff these community centers? Should they be completely staffed by full time doctors and nurses, or could paramedicals and welfare recipients with special training handle the bulk of the routine work load, thus requiring fewer doctors and nurses?
- How should changing work loads affect the budgets of each operation?
- How should the patient loads and budgets change for each institution with the new emphasis on community health centers?
- What are the alternatives and the various possible levels of effort for

each function required by the institutions and community health centers: rehabilitation, professional services, attendants and non-professionals, administrative staff, cleaning, maintenance, laboratory, psychiatric, and so on?

These detailed decisions heavily influence the resources required to provide the services specified by the basic policy decisions of PPB. The first two questions might be addressed by PPB, since they are basic, yet regional differences (such as dispersion of population, transportation) and availability of personnel can heavily affect the actual implementation and resource requirements.

PPB does not provide an operating tool for the line managers who implement the policy and programs and hence does not utilize this huge management resource below the top agency level whose actions have such a significant impact on both program effectiveness and efficiency. PPB has involved more top agency officials in planning and budgeting. But what about all the managers below this top level who implement the policy decisions? They either get handed a budget or they vie among themselves for the largest piece they can get of a predetermined budget figure calculated in the PPB process. These managers are not required to evaluate their operations, have no incentive to be cost effective, and have little satisfaction from actively participating in policy decisions and budget determination.

PPB evaluates alternative ways to achieve a given end, but there are many alternatives and trade-offs available among varying levels of effort for each program as well as alternatives among the many operations and activities in each program. These trade-offs are especially important when the total budget request must balance to some fixed amount, which is the case in most state and local governments that cannot legally go into debt, and whose budget requests must balance to anticipated revenues. Without some type of ranking procedure the budget balancing act becomes a game of juggling many pieces until they equal a given total. Such a juggling act, without the evaluation of varying levels of effort for programs and activities, in no way assures top management that the most important programs and activities are being funded.

PPB focuses primarily on new programs or major increases requested for ongoing programs and hence falls into the same trap as almost all planning and budgeting techniques. PPB will occasionally cause some programs and program elements to be phased out, such as specific military weapons systems, but most government programs are ongoing and are therefore not continually scrutinized. This is especially unfortunate since a major portion of the budget is consumed by these programs. Many activities and operations within each element should be eliminated or reduced because of changing situations but are instead continued at the same or increased levels because the element is continued.

Unfortunately these critical gaps are more significant in state and local government than they are in federal government. State and local governments do not have the same characteristics as the Department of Defense and other massive federal agencies, with their vast organizations and resources, complex interactions among departments, centralized decision making, and significant discretion of the department in allocating resources. State and local agencies do not have this massive size and complexity, and they are restricted in many programs by federal and other guidelines, with local political factors influential in the detailed budgeting and operating levels. State and local governments therefore do not have the same need for a comparably massive planning and program structure, since they tend to view many of their programs as a series of tasks or functions to be performed, with their main need being for a decision making process to determine the best way to efficiently and effectively implement these prescribed tasks and functions.

ZERO-BASE BUDGETING AS IT FILLS THE CRITICAL GAPS AND REINFORCES PPB

Can zero-base budgeting be used with PPB or are the two systems mutually exclusive so that managers must choose between them? We firmly believe that:

- Zero-base budgeting and PPB are compatible.
- Zero-base budgeting fills the critical gaps in PPB.
- Zero-base budgeting reinforces PPB.
- PPB can provide the planning and policy framework required to effectively implement zero-base budgeting.

A marriage of the two systems strengthens both, and PPB and zero-base budgeting can be merged into a coordinated process by changing the concept of budgeting in PPB into zero-base budgeting.

Zero-Base Budgeting Fills the Critical Gaps

To understand how the two systems fit together, we can first look at how zero-base budgeting fills the critical gaps in PPB. Referring to the five gaps listed in the previous section:

1. Zero-base budgeting focuses on how to achieve a given objective.

2. Zero-base budgeting is a detailed evaluation of policy and alternatives in each of the many activities and operations within the program element for which the objective and general policy has been defined.

3. Zero-base budgeting provides an operating tool for the line managers to evaluate their operations, make recommendations as to the most efficient and effective means to achieve their operational objectives, and identify the effect of various funding levels on their operations.

4. Zero-base budgeting provides the mechanism to evaluate the impact of various funding levels on program and program elements. The detailed evaluation of each operation at varying levels can provide the basis to determine both the best implementation plan and the impact of various funding levels on the program elements. This summary evaluation of each element produced by the zero-base budgeting analysis can lead to the evaluations and trade-offs among elements to produce similar evaluations at the program level, and can provide a better basis for determining funding levels among programs.

5. Zero-base budgeting forces managers to review in detail the efficiency and effectiveness of all plans and budgets.

PPB provides the macroeconomic tool for centralized decision making on major policy issues and basic fund allocations. Zero-base budgeting provides the microeconomic tool to transform these objectives into an efficient operating plan and budget and allows managers to evaluate the effect of various funding levels on programs and program elements so that limited resources can be more effectively allocated.

Zero-Base Budgeting Reinforces PPB

Zero-base budgeting reinforces PPB efforts because it provides a solid foundation of information about all functions and operations. This foundation can reinforce and improve PPB efforts in several ways:

- *Program structure.* The evaluation of operations should clearly identify the interactions among operations and thus provide a ready data base from which to develop or modify the program structure.
- *Issue identification.* Operating managers identify many issues and policy questions, questions both specific to their own operations and relating to the overall programs; and the review of decision packages and rankings by central staffs will usually surface additional issues, alternatives, and policy questions as analysts evaluate the impact of the operations on program objectives.

- *Special analysis.* The mass of information and analysis provided by zero-base budgeting offers a ready-made data source for program analysis.
- *Program and financial plans.* Projections, financial data, and program measures should be improved due to the detailed analysis of all activities, with a completely documented evaluation of policy questions and alternatives within each operation.

In addition to improving these aspects of PPB, zero-base budgeting greatly eases the task of those managers and analysts responsible for implementing PPB. One of the major problems in implementing PPB is the lack of a trained staff. A significant portion of the manpower required to implement PPB spends its time digging for the information that can be readily provided by zero-base budgeting. Therefore, zero-base budgeting should greatly reduce the work loads of those responsible for PPB, both in the initial installation and in its continuing use. The information and analyses prepared by the operating managers in zero-base budgeting should also help the central staffs responsible for PPB to a better understanding of operations and operating problems, which should improve their analyses and the probability their analyses will be used.

Merging the Two Systems

When initially presented with the prospect of doing zero-base budgeting in addition to PPB, managers have a tendency to throw up their hands in frustration and claim that they cannot possibly support another system on top of PPB. Several arguments are usually presented to support this contention:

- PPB consumes the entire calendar. How can we possibly add zero-base budgeting, which requires as an input the policy and program decisions determined by PPB?
- How can we use zero-base budgeting on new programs and changes in existing policy when many of these decisions are made at the last minute or by the legislature?
- How can we add zero-base budgeting when our analytic capacity and administrative staffs are already overburdened with PPB?
- How can we be sure that zero-base budgeting will not end up as a dual system with the actual decisions made the way they always have been?

These are legitimate fears of managers who have often had a "new management process that would revolutionize government" shoved down their throats, but these fears can be dispelled.

In the federal government, PPB consumes the entire calendar, with next year's process starting when the current year's appropriation request is completed. This raised an interesting question: Would not the time requirements of PPB force a choice between zero-base budgeting and PPB? The budgeting process in PPB is a cost calculation based on policy and program decisions, which can be done in a much shorter time than zero-base budgeting. Zero-base budgeting, on the other hand, requires these policy and program decisions at the start if the output is to be meaningful.

This timing problem does create conflicts. Referring to the time requirements of zero-base budgeting as indicated in Chapter 7, basic program and policy decisions for programs or elements to be budgeted must be made by late spring or early summer in order to be incorporated into the executive budget recommendation prepared in November and December. Exhibit 8-2 identifies the calendar conflicts that prohibits the use of zero-base budgeting and forces reliance on budget calculations. However, a substantial part of the budget *can* be developed using zero-base budgeting. Some decision packages for new programs, or substantial increases in existing programs where there are no operating managers to prepare detailed activity analyses, may be gross cost estimates that would encompass many activities and operations. However, these cost estimates may be displayed in decision packages, including several levels of effort, and may be incorporated into the rankings along with other packages competing for the same resources. As these new or expanded programs become operational, the zero-base budgeting process may be applied to the discrete activities and operations. There will be some calendar conflicts between PPB and zero-base budgeting that will require budget estimates, but these conflicts can be virtually eliminated in smaller federal agencies and in state and local governments because of their shorter communication lines and quicker response capabilities.

How can zero-base budgeting be used on new programs or changes in existing policy when many of these decisions are made at the last minute or by the legislature? Such last minute changes do necessitate the use of budget estimates or calculations and force management to fall back upon whatever methods they used in the past to handle such changes. However, the zero-base budgeting analyses can provide a better basis from which to make the budget calculations and operating changes. After the funding allocation has been made, agency managers may require some zero-base budgeting efforts in order to effectively

Exhibit 8-2   Calendar Conflicts: Zero-Base Budgeting and PPB

Ongoing programs (including moderate increases)
  Program assumptions and guidelines required by operating managers can be developed by top level agency managers in the early spring. (No calendar conflict. Zero-base budgeting can be used for all operations.)
Major increases in ongoing programs
  Increases from 25 to 75% may be developed by zero-base budgeting. If this increase is generated by increasing current operations, a reasonably detailed evaluation and justification should be expected. If this increase is generated by the creation of new staffs and operations, a much less detailed analysis can be expected since these packages will probably be prepared by administrative staffs. Multiple increases (four and five times the current level) in program levels may require budget calculations since there is no existing operating staff to do zero-base budgeting; however, programs may still be displayed in decision package format, including several levels of effort, and be ranked with the other packages. (Possible calendar conflict. Zero-base budgeting can probably be used to justify most increases, with budget calculations used where necessary.)
New programs
  Initial budgets will probably be determined by budget estimations since no operating staff exists for detailed package preparation. New programs may be displayed in decision packages, with several levels of effort, and ranked with the other packages. As detailed implementation budgets are developed after the funds have been appropriated, zero-base budgeting may be used for internal agency management. Zero-base budgeting can be used in subsequent years for the detailed activity analysis. (Calendar conflict. Budget estimations are required, although these gross estimates may be displayed in package formats and rankings so that the concept and mechanics of zero-base still applies.)
Major changes in ongoing programs
  Use of zero-base budgeting or budget calculations depends on the nature and timing of the changes. If a change is defined early in the planning cycle, and if the change involves policy and procedural shifts without major changes in staffing and functional alignments, zero-base budgeting can be effectively used. (Possible calendar conflict.)
Changes in expenditure levels
  No recycling of budget submissions required for zero-base budgeting inputs; packages can be added or deleted as required (see Chapter 6). (No calendar conflict.)

implement the changes and allocate the appropriate funds. Unfortunately, there is no practical way to achieve complete closure between changing policies and programs and detailed budget analyses and justification in massive organizations.

How can we add zero-base budgeting when analytic and administrative staffs are already overburdened with PPB? We do not believe that zero-base budgeting is an additive system to PPB from a work load standpoint, but rather is a supportive system. The work load of PPB is shouldered primarily by central analytic staffs, whereas the work load of zero-base budgeting is shouldered by operating managers. PPB has required added staffs because budget staffs still had to maintain the normal budget process. This same budget staff can direct the implementation of zero-base budgeting without significant increases in manpower of either the budget staff or staffs responsible for PPB (see Chapter 7). The information and analysis provided by zero-base budgeting should become the basis for program evaluation and summary analyses (see Chapter 5) presented to top management, and should help reduce the work loads on PPB staffs who would be supplied with a great amount of information that they now must develop for themselves. Top management can still concentrate on major changes and new programs, assured that lower level managers have done their jobs in more detailed evaluations of their operations.

How can we be sure that zero-base budgeting will not become a parallel and competitive decision making process (such as PPB has become in many agencies)? PPB became a parallel path in decision making and budgeting because the traditional channels of budgeting were still used—and the method of allocating funds realistically determines the meaningful decision process. This problem can be avoided with zero-base budgeting if it is the only budgeting process used. The use of zero-base budgeting as the budget process should not be difficult to achieve since it meets the needs of operating managers and budgeteers, whereas PPB is not directed at satisfying these microeconomic operating needs.

ZERO-BASE BUDGETING AND GOVERNMENT PLANNING AND BUDGETING

Government has a difficult time in evaluating the effectiveness and efficiency of its programs, for which it lacks the readily definable profit measures that industry enjoys. PPB tries to evaluate the effectiveness or outputs of its programs but often gets bogged down in its efforts to define objectives, measure program impact on the public good, or evaluate increased welfare of society. Statements of objectives have often been a series of unobjectionable homilies that do not provide measures of policy success and program effectiveness, nor do they provide operating guidance to the managers who must implement the programs. Because of these problems, objectives have often become operational, with the differences between means and ends becoming obscure. These real-world problems should not inhibit attempts to improve policy and program analysis, but indicate the desperate need to ensure that these policies and programs are carried out efficiently. PPB is a macroeconomic tool, implemented primarily by top level management and analytic staffs, and aimed primarily at evaluating program effectiveness while only scratching the surface of evaluating the operating and economic efficiency in which programs are implemented. PPB therefore aims at only one side of the problem. The purpose of this chapter was to demonstrate that zero-base budgeting could aim at the other side of the problem, and could be coordinated with or within the PPB framework to simultaneously evaluate effectiveness and efficiency.

Zero-base budgeting taps a large reservoir of program knowledge and analytic resources ignored by PPB—the operating managers throughout the agency hierarchy. The effectiveness of these managers makes or breaks any program in industry or government, and the management benefits of zero-base budgeting identified in Chapter 2 can be achieved in government by effectively directing these available manpower resources. If the top-down efforts of PPB can be coordinated with the predominantly bottom-up efforts of zero-base budgeting, government can take a long step forward toward achieving some of the high expectations initially anticipated from PPB. Zero-base budgeting is still in its infancy, but we believe the process will experience widespread use in federal, state, and local governments, with government using a combination Planning, Programming, and (Zero-Base) Budgeting System.

CHAPTER 9

COMPUTER APPLICATIONS

The computer is an expensive tool, it is not the solution to all management problems, its use does not necessarily indicate sophistication nor does it guarantee quality in the product produced, and may be a burden rather than a benefit. However, the computer can become a tool that makes the difference between failure or success of zero-base budgeting in that it provides management in extremely large organizations with a viable analysis and decision making tool. When thousands of decision packages are produced, zero-base budgeting may grind almost to a halt because top management (or the support staffs that may prepare summaries for top management) cannot manually handle and evaluate the mass of data involved. Management can get so lost in the detailed analyses provided in the decision packages that it loses sight of the overall objective of the operations or programs of which each package represents only one segment of the total, and therefore loses sight of the forest because of the trees. This volume problem may be further compounded if analyses must be continually updated for changes in the packages and rankings. The computer can be an effective tool in solving such volume problems by serving two basic functions:

1. *Mechanical.* Given a weighting or voting on each package, the computer can produce ranking forms, update ranking forms and memory-stored data for revisions in packages and priorities, and absorb the large volume of data from the packages and rankings.
2. *Analytical.* The computer can provide numerical analyses on the large volumes of data to aid top management in evaluating the decision packages, rankings, and the effectiveness of various organizations or programs at different funding levels.

This chapter identifies some computer applications that can aid

159

management in solving the volume problems as well as some applications that can lead toward a total information system. This discussion is divided into three sections:

1. *Applications.* Mechanical and analytical applications that can aid management in effectively utilizing the zero-base budgeting process.
2. *General systems specifications.* General specifications for systems designed to implement the applications identified, including possible input sources and a sample output format.
3. *Toward a total information system.* Future directions and possibilities to provide management with a comprehensive planning, budgeting, control, reporting, and information system.

Small organizations developing only a few hundred packages may never have any use for these computer applications and should consider themselves lucky. Large organizations may be forced to use computer aids. One of the descisions a large organization must make when initially implementing zero-base budgeting is whether computer aids are needed, and if so what type of system is necessary or desirable. Hopefully, this discussion of some general computer applications, along with the discussions in other chapters concerning the problems each organization may have in implementing zero-base budgeting, will help each organization to make this decision. However, elaborate systems efforts should be avoided the first year, with the effort limited to those programs required to survive any volume problems. In subsequent years, management will be better equipped to design and implement an effective computer system—after it has been through the process, experienced the problems involved, and actually seen the potential management tool that the mass of information contained in the decision packages and rankings can provide if properly used.

With these words of caution, we can proceed to the discussion of possible computer applications, which can play a significant supporting role in the effective and efficient implementation of zero-base budgeting in large organizations.

APPLICATIONS

The computer applications discussed in this section are intended to identify some of the mechanical and analytical solutions that the computer can provide to aid management in effectively utilizing the zero-base budgeting process. These applications are not all-inclusive since each organization has its own particular problems and needs, but hopefully the applications identified will provide a background and a starting point from which managers can design their own systems. There are seven possible applications identified in this section:

1. Ranking
2. Analysis of rankings and trends
3. Program analysis
4. Revisions in packages and priorities
5. "What if" capabilities
6. Analysis of common functions and work measures
7. Detail budgeting and accounting

The use of a computer may not be justified for any single application; however, several of these applications are closely associated, and the implementation of one application requires only minor additions to incorporate several additional applications.

Ranking

To rank a large number of decision packages, an individual or committee will probably assign a weight or vote to each package as it is initially reviewed. This preliminary ranking will then be analyzed (see the following section on computer applications for the analysis of rankings and trends), with the rankings altered as required to produce the final ranking. This procedure, with some possible weighting and voting scales, is discussed in Chapter 5. The mechanical task of preparing these rankings and producing the ranking sheets can become a clerical headache, conducive to clerical errors, and can delay the review of and revisions to the preliminary ranking. The clerical problem is compounded if a committee is used since the votes must be tabulated, with additional time delays if there are multiple voting criteria.

The computer can offer a quick turnaround solution to this problem, performing the following tasks:

1. Tabulating the weights or votes assigned to each package by an individual or committee.
2. Sorting the packages in order of highest assigned priority.
3. Printing the ranking sheet, with the computer numbering the packages in the ranking, tabulating cumulative expenditures, calculating the percent of current year's expense, and so on.

If the computer is preloaded with all the information needed to produce the ranking form, and if the votes are fed into the computer during the ranking session, the preliminary ranking can be produced almost immediately after the last package has been voted upon. This rapid turnaround allows the managers to review and revise their preliminary rankings the same day, while the packages are still fresh in their minds.

Analysis of Rankings and Trends

The initial evaluation of most rankings starts with an analysis of the changes that take place in the expenditure level of each activity at various funding levels in the final ranking. Managers will want to evaluate the addition of new activities, elimination of current activities, and significant increases or decreases in expenditure levels by budget unit, program, or any other organizational consolidation, for both dollars and people, and at several levels of funding. Management can use this quantitative trend evaluation as the starting point in the evaluation of the rankings, determining the desirability of various expenditure levels, program efficiency and effectiveness, and so on. The computer can be effective in making this quantitative analysis by performing the following functions (given a ranking and the appropriate historical data):

1. Priorities established by the ranking can be identified. At specified funding levels wtihin a given ranking, managers can see the changes in dollar and people levels among budget units or other organizational groupings. For example, to analyze the final consolidated ranking for the organization shown in Exhibit 1-5 in Chapter 1, we might analyze the ranking at the 80, 100, and 110% expenditure levels. At the 80% funding level for A, B_1 might be funded at 50%, B_2 funded at 95%, and B_3 funded at 85%. Looking at each budget unit, we might find D_1 not funded at all, D_2 funded at 150%, and D_3 funded at 70%. We can then analyze the 100 and 110% funding levels for A and evaluate the relative shifts in priorities between the various funding levels on each organizational unit.

2. Trend analysis and package listings can be made for special organizational groupings to facilitate analysis. The fragmentation of each activity into several decision packages can make it difficult to evaluate the impact of the packages and rankings on the budget units, programs, or other organizational units. Taking the decision packages and rankings as presented in one or several consolidated rankings, the computer

can sort them into meaningful organizational units so that management can evaluate the impact of the packages on the output and effectiveness of these units at various funding levels.

3. Special analyses can be made on specific categories of operations and costs. For example, nonrepetitive costs such as capital expenditures (in governmental organizations where a capital expenditure is treated as a period cost) can be isolated from the historical data, with the decision packages for all capital expenditures isolated, so that package listings and trend analyses can be made for (a) all expenditures, (b) expenditures excluding capital, and (c) capital expenditures.

4. Cost estimates can be reviewed for reasonableness by historical comparison of costs and people. If detailed costing is shown on each package, the computer can prepare trend analyses on each category of expense, calculate average salaries and wages or cost per person, and so on.

5. Management can readily ascertain if proper emphasis has been placed on specific activities and programs. For example, mental hospitals and prisons may want to emphasize rehabilitation, yet rankings might bring the administrative and maintenance functions back to their current level of effort before any rehabilitation packages are ranked. This political ploy of identifying important programs to be cut if fund requests are reduced would be a great way to justify additional funds if the priorities were not analyzed and challenged.

These analyses can be performed mechanically without the aid of the computer. However, large organizations that create thousands of decision packages, with constant changes in the packages and rankings, can usurp its analytical capacity in performing mechanical manipulations of data, and may have no practical alternative other than the computer.

Program Analysis

To effectively evaluate the decision packages and rankings to establish a funding level, we must evaluate these packages and rankings relative to their ability to achieve a predetermined set of goals and objectives. This task is often complicated because the goals and objectives are identified for a program, but we may not achieve one consolidated ranking for each program. We may not achieve this ranking for one of two major reasons:

1. The number of decision packages exceeds management's ability to produce a single consolidated ranking for the program.

2. The program may cut across organizational boundaries, either by design or historical accident, so that:

(a) There may be no formal organizational structure for the program, and therefore no organizational hierarchy to rank the packages for a given program.

(b) Top management may play the role of arbitrator and decision maker for fund allocations, making funding decisions on each of several separate rankings submitted by the organizations participating in the program.

This problem is common in government (see Chapter 8 on PPB), and occasionally in industry. Government is often faced with unwieldy organizations because its structure was determined by historical accident through legislation passed over a number of years. In the State of Georgia, we coded a program structure on top of the normal organization structure so that we could bring together the decision packages and rankings for each program. For example, the activities for the program of "Crime Prevention and Control" were spread among several agencies:

Activity	Agency
Arson investigation and arrest	Comptroller General
Drug abuse prevention and education	Pharmacy Board
Georgia Bureau of Investigation	Public Safety
Crime laboratory	Public Safety
Georgia prison system	Corrections
Youth development and detention centers	Family and Children Services
Pardons and paroles	Pardons and Parole Board
Probation supervision	Probation Board

Industry does not usually have as great a problem because most organizations are structured along product lines. (Most product lines are really programs, with goals and objectives set in terms of market penetration, sales, profit, etc.) However, industry will often have common service and support programs in each division that it wishes to coordinate across the entire organization, such as research and development, personnel, or management systems. Top management may want to review all packages for these programs for consistency, and to ensure that the varying profit pictures among divisions do not cause some high priority packages to the corporation to go unfunded in a division with a tight profit picture while lower priority packages get funded in another division with a bright profit picture.

The computer can aid management in evaluating the separate rankings and bringing together the program elements from the separate organizations. This may be done by superimposing a program structure on top of the normal organization structure. Such an organizational structure might be as follows:

Organizational Coding

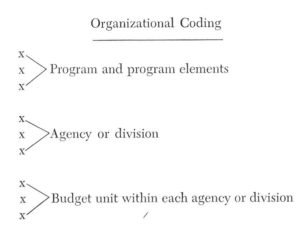

X
x > Program and program elements
X

X
x > Agency or division
X

X
x > Budget unit within each agency or division
X

Such an organizational coding will allow the computer to bring together all the packages for each program and to create the type of analysis of rankings and trends discussed in the previous section. The rankings displayed in this structure will reflect those established within each organizational ranking, whether the packages for a given program are in a separate ranking or merged with other packages from each organization. Top management can then review and alter the priorities established in each agency or division and establish the relative priorities and funding levels for the program elements in each organization to produce the program budget.

Revisions in Packages and Priorities

During the zero-base budgeting process, there will usually be continual changes in packages and rankings, which can cause continuous updates in ranking forms and analyses. The computer can be used effectively to readily handle all changes in packages and rankings and all updating of analyses by performing the following tasks:

1. Revising the rankings by identifying the packages involved and specifying the desired position in the ranking.
2. Adding decision packages and specifying the desired priority.
3. Deleting decision packages and having all following packages move up to fill the gap.
4. Changing any package information, such as costs, people, name.

These updates can be made periodically or continuously, with the capability of making all updates during one revision cycle.

"What If" Capabilities

During the decision making process, top management has three basic needs for "what if" capabilities:

1. The funding levels among many agencies, divisions, or separate rankings may have to be balanced out to equal anticipated revenues or a desired expenditure level.
2. Allowable expenditure levels may change during the budget process, and top management can specify these changes by determining new cutoff levels for any or all rankings.
3. Top management may want to establish an acceptable funding range for each ranking, and continually modify the desired funding cutoff level within this range as the profit picture changes or as additional reviews update and alter management thinking.

In Chapter 5 we saw the computer application that the Governor of Georgia used to play "what if" to balance funding levels among 65 agencies against anticipated revenues. For this application, four levels of funding were identified:

Level 1. Minimum level of funding recommended. If the minimum level of funding were approved for all rankings, the total funding would be less than anticipated revenues or would cause profit goals to be exceeded.

Level 2. "What if" (tentative) level within the recommended funding range. Management can continually modify this level, which will eventually become the approved funding level for all rankings.

Level 3. Maximum level of funding recommended. If the maximum level were approved for each ranking, the total funding would exceed anticipated revenues or would cause profits to be reduced below goal levels.

Level 4. Total funds requested. This level might already have been limited by some expenditure guidelines.

These levels were specified by the number of packages contained in each level—that is, either level 1 included packages 1–100, level 2 included packages 1–125, level 3 included packages 1–150, and level 4 included all packages in the ranking; or the level could also be specified by the percent of the prior year's expenditure level—that is, level 1 included all packages within the 80% level, level 2 included all within the 90% level, and so on. At each level, the computer performed the analyses previously discussed.

Analysis of Common Functions and Work Measures

There are many common functions performed in different organizational units, as well as duplicate organizational and activity frameworks for decentralized operations such as hospitals or manufacturing facilities. Common functions might include cleaning, maintenance, record keeping, production planning, training, supervision, industrial engineering, marketing, management systems, nursing (in hospitals), or food service. The decision package helps management to identify these common functions and allows management to analyze the effectiveness of the various operations through cost analysis and quantitative work measure analysis displayed on the packages.

The computer can aid in two aspects of this analysis:

1. The computer can identify all decision packages for any specified function(s).

2. The computer can analyze and compare the common work measures for these specified functions.

A manual search can be done reasonably quickly by reviewing the ranking sheets, but this forces the analyst to rely on the package name to provide an adequate description to identify the specific function(s) he is looking for. Further, the analyst must still find the package in order to take the pertinent data and put them into a workable format for his analysis.

To develop this computer application, a master list of common functions and quantitative measures for each function needs to be developed. This list of functions can be provided with the zero-base budgeting instructions, with each manager required to identify the standard quantitative measures specified for that function. The appropriate packages can then be coded to reflect a given function, with the appropriate coding and quantitative measures displayed on each package. This is a relatively simple task after zero-base budgeting has been done once or twice since the functional analysis provided by the packages should be reasonably detailed by that time, and management should have a firm basis to identify those functions and work measures they want analyzed on a standard basis.

Detail Budgeting and Accounting

The computer systems used in zero-base budgeting should feed into the computerized budgeting and accounting control systems used during the operating year. If the decision package format shows monthly or quarterly cost information, and/or cost breakdown by line item of expense or chart of accounts, this information can be taken from the approved decision packages to produce the detailed budgets required for each budget unit and consolidation level. In many instances, the detail budgeting by month or quarter and the chart of accounts will be done after the funding decisions have been made. In this case, the computer program will merely provide the yearly dollar totals and the positions approved for the budget units and consolidation levels, and the additional detail must then be added to the system. The computer output can also be formatted to produce any budget documents required. For example, the numerical data displayed in the executive budget recommendations submitted to the state legislatures in most states can be produced by the computer.

GENERAL SYSTEMS SPECIFICATIONS

This section identifies some of the general systems specifications that should be helpful in designing a system to encompass some or all computer applications discussed, or to expand an initial system that merely handles the volume problem into a more complex analytical system. Several general needs should be addressed in designing a computer system for the applications discussed:

1. A common system is needed for general use throughout the organization. Managers within each large agency or division have the same needs and problems—to a somewhat lesser degree—as top management, and these agency or division managers can use the computer

as a working tool in addition to providing the analyses and summaries required.

2. The computer inputs of decision package and ranking data for internal agency and division use should provide the data base and feed the program used by top management for intra-agency analysis.

3. The initial systems design should be flexible and open ended for future expansion to include additional analysis or feed into the budgeting/accounting control systems used during the operating year.

4. Top management may require that each agency or division input the appropriate information into the computer system for intra-agency analysis, but each agency or division should determine the level within its own organization at which it becomes meaningful to use the computer system.

5. Decision package information may be put into a permanent file with a unique identification number. If package information is entered at a low organizational level, a permanent identification number can facilitate identification as the package ranking changes at various consolidation levels. The rank number thus becomes a variable within the permanent file on each package.

6. Historical data and budget decisions should be retained on file for use in the following year's computer applications and analyses.

The greatest problem in designing a system for zero-base budgeting is that of handling several rankings as each package proceeds from its initial ranking at a low organization level to its ultimate ranking at the highest consolidation level. There is also the problem of handling general revisions of package data and selective revisions to any established ranking. This problem can be readily circumvented by using the permanent identification number for each package as described, with the computer doing the physical ranking and numbering of packages at each ranking level (given management's weighting or voting on each package), The program can also be designed to handle the ranking shortcuts identified in Chapter 5.

Data Input

One need of any computer system involving large amounts of data is getting the data into the computer efficiently and cheaply. To implement the applications described, the computer system will require file data and historical information (organization structure, codes, names, historical data on expenditures, people, quantitative package measures) as well as the active data input for the decision packages and rankings. There are three possible sources from which the package and ranking information can initially be input into the computer:

1. Ranking form
2. Decision package form
3. Special input documents

The ranking and decision package forms, if properly designed, can be the source documents for computer input and have an advantage over special input documents since the package and ranking forms are an integral part of the zero-base budgeting process.

The ranking form provides the easiest source of input since it contains the basic package information for numerous packages, but it also limits the amount of information that can be processed. However, the form can be designed with spaces for special codings, or a separate sheet can be attached to provide additional information on each package for computer input. Nevertheless, the decision package form itself offers the best source for data input since it contains all available information and does not require the copying of additional information onto any ranking or special input documents solely for the purpose of computer input.

The additional work required to make the computer codings and inputs can be done by a clerical staff at some administrative level within each division or agency. The operating manager preparing the packages need not be confused or involved with any special codings or computer requirements and need only know that there are several spaces on the form that he should leave blank for computer codes.

Output Formats

There are many possible output formats, but these formats will probably fall into one of (or be a combination of) two basic categories:

1. Numerical analysis. Trend or comparative analysis on any information contained in the decision package files for any organizational unit specified.

2. Package listings. Computer listings of decision packages and package information for any organizational unit or function specified.

Exhibit 9-1 shows a trend analysis for the Health Agency, with the Agency broken down by program, and each program broken down by activity or department (and each activity broken down into lower organizational units if desired). The four budget levels were specified as a percentage of the current year's funding level in state dollars for the Agency, with level 4 specified at some arbitrarily high level so that it will include all decision packages (level 4 turns out to be 126% in this example). This analysis shows that at the 100% funding level for the Agency in state dollars (level 2), Environmental Health is funded at 98%, and Health Surveillance and Disease Control is funded at only 90%.

Exhibit 9-2 shows a decision package listing for all the sanitation packages within the Health Agency's ranking. The rank number is the final rank number of each package within the 1400 packages in the total agency ranking (which we later concluded was far too many for a single ranking), and the cumulative dollars and percents show activity totals. If we review Exhibits 9-1 and 9-2 jointly, we can see which packages are included within each funding level for sanitation. In Exhibit 9-1, we can see that at level 2 sanitation is funded at $920,000 or 97% state dollars, with Exhibit 9-2 showing that packages through number 600 are included in that level. With this numerical analysis and package display, we can begin to evaluate in detail the effect of this funding level on the operations and output of sanitation and its effect on the Environmental Health Program.

These same formats can be used in program analyses that cut across agency lines, or used to produce the activity analysis that breaks each activity down into its various consolidation levels and budget units, and used to consolidate the figures from all agencies or programs to produce a summary analysis for the organization as a whole. These two basic formats can be used for a common computer system throughout an organization for ranking, analysis of ranking and trends, program analysis, revisions in packages and priorities, and "what if" capabilities.

TOWARD A TOTAL INFORMATION SYSTEM

The dream of the systems designer is to develop a computer system or network of systems to provide all levels of management with all information and analysis required for decision making and effective management of the operations. Zero-base budgeting is the missing link in most current management information and decision making systems in that it provides a detailed analysis on all activities and operations

Exhibit 9-1   Trend Analysis (Agency: Health)

COSTS INCLUDING CAPITAL OUTLAY AND AUTHORITY LEASE RENTALS—
IN THOUSANDS OF DOLLARS

AGENCY BUDGET TREND

	FY 69	FY 70	%	FY 71	%	FY 72	%	LEVEL 2/ FY 73	%
TOTAL DOLLARS	150,995	171,150	113	252,657	148	290,633	115	301,546	104
STATE DOLLARS	77,181	97,509	126	138,392	142	160,194	116	160,112	100
NO. OF PEOPLE	8,570	10,323	120	11,492	111	11,797	103	9,686	82

* *

STATE FUNDING LEVEL: LEVEL 1 = 080%, LEVEL 2 = 100%, LEVEL 3 = 105%, LEVEL 4 = 999%

* *

AGENCY TOTALS:

	FY 71	FY 72	%	FY 73 LEVEL 1	%	LEVEL 2	%	LEVEL 3	%	LEVEL 4	%
TOTAL $	252,657	290,633	115	233,509	80	301,546	104	309,709	107	352,222	121
STATE $	138,392	160,194	116	128,112	80	160,112	100	167,993	105	201,306	126
PEOPLE	11,492	11,797	103	8,598	73	9,686	82	10,219	87	12,942	110

* *

PROGRAM: ENVIRONMENTAL HEALTH

TOTAL $	947	1,024	108	1,068	104	1,185	116	1,282	125	1,782	174
STATE $	906	1,024	113	885	86	1,002	98	1,099	107	1,599	156
PEOPLE	73	73	100	67	92	76	104	83	114	117	160

ACTIVITY (DEPARTMENT): SANITATION

TOTAL $	963	946	110	986	104	1,103	117	1,200	127	1,700	180
STATE $	832	946	114	803	85	920	97	1,017	108	1,517	160
PEOPLE	69	69	100	63	91	72	104	79	114	113	164

(OTHER ACTIVITIES WITHIN THE ENVIRONMENTAL HEALTH PROGRAM)

PROGRAM: HEALTH SURVEILLANCE AND DISEASE CONTROL

TOTAL $	8,358	8,403	101	7,093	84	7,977	95	7,977	95	10,968	131
STATE $	6,879	7,102	103	5,579	79	6,396	90	6,396	90	9,275	131
PEOPLE	830	827	100	586	71	668	81	668	81	1,016	123

Exhibit 9-2 Decision Package Listing (Activity: Sanitation)

RANK	DECISION PACKAGE NAME	SEQ NUMBER	FY 72 TOTAL $	FY 72 STATE $	PEOPLE	TOTAL $	FY 73 STATE $	PEOPLE	CUM-73 TOTAL $	CUM-73 STATE $	CUM %
119	DIRECT SUPPORT BRANCH OF SANITATION	1 OF 3	113	113	7	35	35	2	35	35	4
120	DIRECT SUPPORT ENV SANITATION		27	27	2	28	28	2	63	63	7
121	DIRECT SUPPORT SOLID WASTE MNGMT	1 OF 2	33	33	4	40	35	4	103	98	10
122	DIRECT SUPPORT WATER SUPPLY SERVICE		35	35	3	41	41	3	144	139	15
123	DIRECT SUPPORT HOUS & INSTI SAN	1 OF 2	35	35	3	38	38	3	182	177	19
124	WATER SUPPLY CONSTRUCTION	1 OF 2	48	48	3	65	65	4	247	242	26
125	WATER SUPPLY LABORATORY	1 OF 2	120	120	12	163	163	12	410	405	43
126	WATER SUPPLY OPERATION	1 OF 2	53	53	3	55	55	3	465	460	49
127	IND WATER SUPPLY & IND SEWAGE	1 OF 2	42	42	3	34	34	2	499	494	52
128	CLASS III PUBLIC OR COM WATER	1 OF 2	15	15	1	16	16	1	515	510	54
129	ENV SAN OF TOURIST ACC & RECR	1 OF 3	69	69	5	44	44	3	559	554	59
130	FOOD SANITATION	1 OF 2	58	58	4	45	45	3	604	599	63

131	SOLID WASTE MANAGEMENT	1 OF 4	120	120	7	166	55	8	770	654	69
132	SOLID WASTE MANAGEMENT	2 OF 4				132	65	7	902	719	76
133	DIRECT SUPPORT BRANCH OF SANIT	2 OF 3				30	30	2	932	749	79
134	SPECIAL SERVICES	1 OF 2	50	50	4	54	54	4	986	803	85
598	SCHOOL SANITATION	1 OF 2	33	33	2	37	37	2	1,023	840	89
599	ENVR SAN TOURIST ACC & REC AREAS	2 OF 3				43	43	3	1,066	883	93
600	WATER SUPPLY LAB ANALYSIS SAN	2 OF 2				37	37	4	1,103	920	97
746	WATER SUPPLY OPR SANITATION	2 OF 2				25	25	2	1,128	945	100
747	WATER SUPPLY CONST SECT SANITATION	2 OF 2				27	27	2	1,155	972	103
749	SOLID WASTE MGM SANITATION	3 OF 4				45	45	3	1,200	1,017	108
1380	RESIDENTIAL ENVIRONMENT SANITATION	2 OF 2				51	51	4	1,662	1,479	156
1381	INDIVIDUAL WATER SUPP & SEW DISPOSAL	2 OF 2				11	11	1	1,673	1,490	158
1383	PESTICIDE MONITORING SANITATION	1 OF 1				27	27	1	1,700	1,517	160

rather than on just the changes from the current operating and expenditure levels, and it allows us to take a long step toward a total information system. We can take this step by developing and coordinating three basic systems applications:

1. Zero-base budgeting systems. Planning, budgeting, and analysis of all activities and operations for management review and decision making, producing budgets and work measure and performance data against which the operations can be measured.

2. Budgeting/accounting control systems. Detail operating systems reflecting detail budgeting by chart of accounts and monthly or quarterly cost allocations, accumulation and reporting of actual costs during the operating year, and the initial identification of variances between actual and budgeted costs.

3. Management reporting systems. Operational reporting and analysis that highlights problem areas to top management for review and decision making on corrective action, which might include such features as expenditure forecasting, variance analysis on actual and forecast costs as compared to the budget and earlier forecasts, and reporting of actual work measure and performance data against those measures identified on the decision packages.

Such a system would provide management with a viable operating tool. The computer capabilities and technology exist today for the design, implementation, and integration of the three systems as described; but the cost of designing, implementing, maintaining, and operating such a system becomes rapidly prohibitive as we complicate the system in the attempt to provide all the information that management needs. However, as we continue to develop systems to handle operational and work load data in addition to accounting data, and as computer capabilities and technology become more sophisticated so that all information displayed on the decision package form and other source documents becomes machine readable and digestable for analysis purposes, we can begin to come much closer to that mythical total information system.

CHAPTER 10

ZERO-BASE BUDGETING AND THE MANAGEMENT PROCESS

Zero-base budgeting is more than the traditional budgeting process that produces a set of resource allocations in the form of dollar and people numbers for specified organizational units. Zero-base budgeting goes beyond these limited boundaries to provide management with an operating tool to adjust the organization to meet the need and demands of its environment. The previous chapters have focused on the impact that this budgeting has on the planning and budgeting aspects of the management process. This chapter describes how it affects the entire management process, concentrating on the impact that it has on implementation and control, and identifies the impact that zero-base budgeting has on management's continuous effort to improve operations and profitability.

THE MANAGEMENT PROCESS

Zero-base budgeting affects all aspects of the management process, providing managers with an additional operating tool to more effectively manage their business. The four basic components of this process (planning, budgeting, implementation, and control) are an integrated series of events as illustrated in Exhibit 10-1. Management may be fortunate enough to operate in a relatively static environment, where the basic assumptions and planning guidelines remain constant during the planning and budgeting process and prove to be reasonably accurate as compared to the actual situation experienced during the operating year. With reasonable fluctuations in the external and internal operating environment, managers can readily adjust their operations for these fluctuations and can control any programmed modifications through allow-

177

Exhibit 10-1 The Management Process

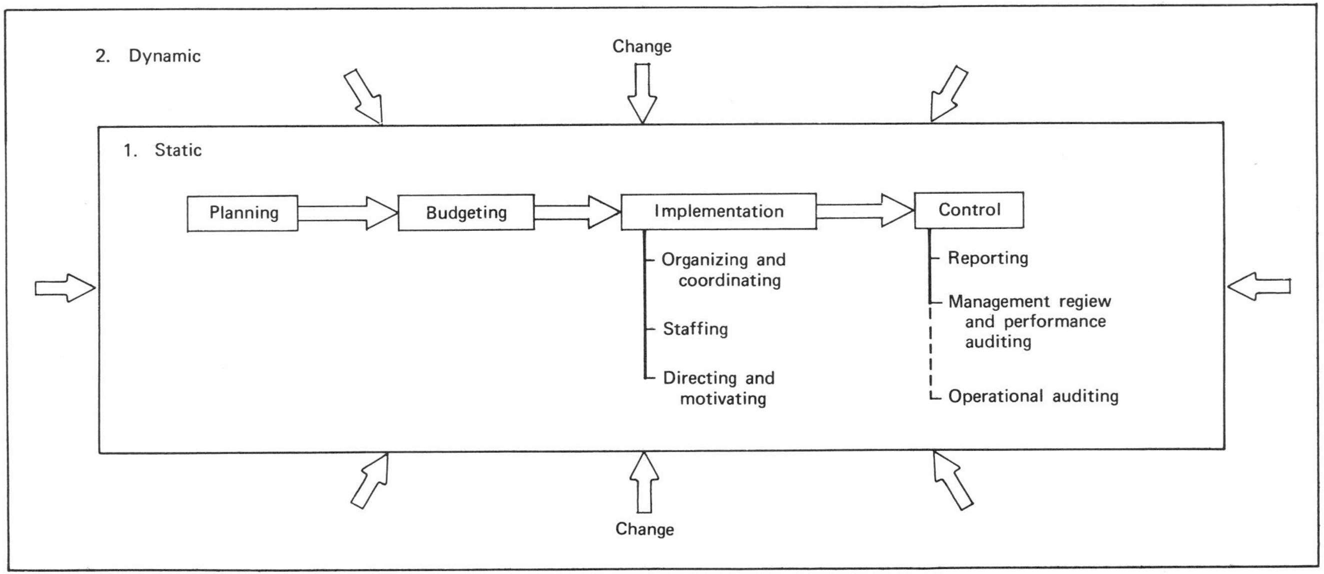

2. Dynamic

1. Static

Planning → Budgeting → Implementation → Control

Implementation
— Organizing and coordinating
— Staffing
— Directing and motivating

Control
— Reporting
— Management regiew and performance auditing
— Operational auditing

Change

able budget variances. However, changes in the external environment beyond some acceptable or manageable limits, or substantial internal operating problems or changes in personnel, force management to react in a dynamic environment that may continually change. In such a case management may be forced to completely revise its plans and budgets, implement major changes to current activities or establish new programs and operations, and revise its controls to meet the new operating situation and criteria.

Static Environment

Zero-base budgeting provides a detailed operating plan and budget for a specified set of circumstances and a desired output. If the environment adheres to the predictions or assumptions made during the planning and budgeting process, the detailed analysis of all activities provides a roadmap for management to follow in implementing the specified plan and budget. Zero-base budgeting impacts all the elements of implementation. The process requires management to evaluate its organizational structure and to identify the interrelationships among activities and organizational units, and readily identifies the overhead costs and operating problems associated with excessively broad or deep organizational structures. The evaluation of the costs and benefits of this administrative overhead as opposed to other activities often leads to a paring or streamlining of the organizational structure to reduce costs and/or improve effectiveness. The definition of relationships between manufacturing operations and its service and support activities is essential to ensure smooth manufacturing operations, especially if volume fluctuates or the same facilities produce a variation of products (whether these fluctuations are planned or unplanned).

The organization's staffing requirements and people budgets for those activities using zero-base budgeting are determined by the summation of people numbers from the approved decision packages. In addition to establishing the number of people in each activity, the packages usually identify the types of people and general duties or activities involved. This information can aid personnel departments in determining hiring needs, establishing a "manpower inventory" of the types of people within the organization, and establishing job descriptions. Management can determine many of its staffing problems during the decision making process as it ranks the packages. Packages for current operations (and people) ranked below the anticipated funding level indicate that these people need to be transferred or laid off. Packages for new activities given a high priority indicate hiring needs or openings that can be filled internally. At the end of the planning and budgeting, top management can get a complete reading of manpower shortages and overages from across the organization and can establish its policies to bring staffing needs and availability into balance.

Zero-base budgeting also aids managers in directing and motivating employees since most managers and their subordinates will have worked together in developing and evaluating the decision packages and operating plans. In many cases, with typical planning and budgeting techniques, managers do not have the opportunity to identify operating problems and needs nor to make their recommendations to top management. Zero-base budgeting provides such a mechanism and also commits managers to a set of defined goals and objectives, performance standards, and accomplishments that they will be held accountable for. The identification and evaluation of each activity is especially helpful for managers assuming new responsibilities, since the packages and rankings provide a ready access library describing and analyzing the duties and commitments of each activity.

Zero-base budgeting allows management to hold all activities and operations to a budget as well as to the performance that each one commits to in its decision packages. The summation of approved packages for each cost center or budget unit provides the budget framework for the reporting of actual costs and budget variances. The analysis provided by each decision package is usually a much deeper analysis of a cost center (which may contain several activities or programs) than previously existed, and aids management in evaluating the reason for cost or performance variances. Typical reporting systems that indicate only cost and people variances from budget or the previous forecast can be augmented by the standard reporting of work load and performance measures for those service and support activities having readily definable measures.

Unfortunately, many of the overhead, service, and support activities using zero-base budgeting do not have readily measurable work load and performance measures that lend themselves to a standard reporting format. The evaluation and control of these activities is not determined by budget variances (which can usually be readily controlled by varying the staffing levels) but by the performance and effectiveness of these activities. Management can determine the performance and effectiveness of these activities through special reviews or performance auditing. At Texas Instruments, for example, the support organizations in the Staff and Research divisions had at least one special review with top management in addition to the normal review of budget and forecast variances to review activities in detail. With the advent of zero-base budgeting, these reviews often started with a review of the approved packages for each organization, and then proceeded with a status report on actual accomplishments versus commitment, problems, corrective action proposed or being undertaken, new programs, and changes in the environment or organizational requirements that were not anticipated in the operating plan and budget. In addition to such a review, performance auditing can be conducted by individual managers or teams of managers, or by an internal audit staff as part of their normal audit procedures.

Operational auditing is rapidly becoming a standard function in management control and is often a formal function of the Internal Auditing Department. Operational auditing aims primarily at improving operations and profits rather than merely verifying costs or evaluating performance against some standard or commitment. This control activity will be discussed in detail in a following section of this chapter.

Dynamic Environment

Zero-base budgeting provides a powerful operating tool for management to adjust operations and resources to keep abreast of a rapidly changing environment. Zero-base budgeting provides three assets that enable management to makes these adjustments:

1. A well analyzed and documented base (or budget) with an existing set of priorities from which management can determine the actions required.
2. An efficient procedure for management to follow to identify the specific actions required, including changes in the assumptions and guidelines during the planning and budgeting process, budget reductions, variable budgeting, and organizational changes (see Chapter 6).
3. A detailed identification of the consequences of the actions taken, with the procedure assuring management that the least important activities were eliminated or reduced.

If the required changes result from cost overruns or developing new activities and programs, zero-base budgeting allows management to review the previously budgeted activities to determine if they should be reduced to provide the funding required.

Major changes implemented using zero-base budgeting techniques have the same foundation for implementation and control of the revised plans and budgets as the original process provided for the original plans and budgets. Reductions based on eliminating or revising decision packages merely revise the road map for management to follow in implementing the revised plan, and allow holding of all activities and operations to a revised budget and a revised set of work load and performance measures. The detailed reductions allow management to identify organization changes, changes in services provided by service and support activities, and the consequences of such changes. Staffing reductions are identified in detail, and the Personnel Department can use its manpower inventory and job descriptions to shuffle personnel among operations to minimize layoffs and keep the best people. The negative impact on motivation and morale can also be minimized because managers can see that the reductions made were in proportion to organization priorities and needs, with each operation's goals and objectives revised in accordance with the revised budget.

THE CONTINUOUS EFFORT TO IMPROVE OPERATIONS AND PROFITABILITY (OPERATIONAL AUDITING)

No budgeting or planning system can expect to solve all of management's problems, which may be long range or deeply entrenched. Although zero-base budgeting will not provide the immediate solution to all problems, the process does provide a great deal of data and analysis that should help to surface or highlight both short-term and long range problems, and force management to reevaluate operations that may have become obsolete or inefficient over the years. The zero-base budgeting process itself is confined within a period of one to several months, while management problems and efforts to improve operations and profitability are ongoing. The formal management effort to improve operations and profitability is sometimes referred to as operational auditing, and zero-base budgeting can play a significant role in this effort.

Operational auditing is a review and appraisal of the effectiveness and efficiency of operations and operating procedures. Its purpose is to complement the normal information and control systems by supplying top management with an appraisal of operations, with emphasis on assisting management in problem solving and increasing profits by recommending realistic courses of action. Operational auditing is often confused with financial auditing because of the term auditing in its title, but there is a decided difference. Financial auditing is primarily concerned with accounting, financial systems, and control, with the main benefit to the organization being protection of assets and verification of financial information. Where this traditional financial auditing is concerned with *verification* of profits, operational auditing is concerned with *increasing* profits; where financial auditing concentrates on the *past,* operational auditing concentrates on the *future;* where financial auditing stresses *fact-finding,* operational auditing stresses *problem solving;* and where financial auditing is normally limited to *financial and control* activities, operational auditing encompasses the *entire spectrum* of an organziation's activities.

Operational auditing is not an organizational entity but is an ongoing method or philosophy of analysis by management. Operational auditing may be performed by several types of participants:

1. Internal to the organization
   - Individual managers
   - Management teams
   - Internal audit departments
   - Central analytic staffs
2. External to the organization
   - Management service and consulting firms
   - Public accounting firms
3. Combinations of the above

The nature of each audit and the internal capabilities of each organization dictate the participants required. Because of the ongoing nature of management's problems in today's dynamic environment, many large organizations are developing permanent in-house capabilities to perform operational auditing, which may be assigned to internal audit departments or centralized corporate and/or division analytic staffs.

The need for ongoing management analyses and operational auditing is created by the arm's-length management required by decentralization in medium size and large organizations, plus the general lack of control or management indicators to identify profit potential. Management obtains the information it needs to operate and control its business in many ways. Sales forecasts, quotas, and reports enable management to assess its marketing activities; operating budgets enable it to assess the cost effectiveness of its manufacturing department; and cost control and progress reports enable it to keep abreast of day-to-day operations. Yet, whether management realizes it or not, such information developed by the normal control and communication channels may be grossly insufficient to enable management to approach optimum profitability. Top management cannot always be sure that information received is accurate and complete, and management may not realize that past inefficiencies may still be reflected in current budgets and cost standards. Nor do any of these tools necessarily measure the performance of staff and support groups or help management keep abreast of changing technology and product development.

Zero-base budgeting goes much deeper and further into operations than do other such techniques to help solve some of the problems of arm's-length management. However, in many cases zero-base budgeting only scratches the surface of a problem area or indicates that a problem may exist. Management must then employ its analytic resources to investigate in detail and resolve the problem, with the investigation or operational audit taking place during the budget process or the operating year. For example, the zero-base budgeting analysis of maintenance may indicate rapidly rising maintenance costs, unfavorable trends of maintenance costs to production volume, or an unfavorable cost comparison between a maintenance activity in one plant and a similar activity in another plant. In a large or complex manufacturing operation, the maintenance activity itself can be large and complex and have a significant impact on the manufacturing operations that is not reflected in the maintenance budget or reporting system. To investigate and rectify any deep-rooted or complex problems, management must often assign additional manpower to the task since such problems may not be completely evaluated or resolved during the normal course of events or the budget process.

In performing an operational audit on the maintenance function, management might discover that the maintenance department has a large backlog of work requests that lacked any evaluation as to need or timing; that maintenance materials were not being adequately controlled, with the result that there were excessively high inventories of many spare parts—some of which had become obsolete; that the preventive maintenance program was not adequate or well controlled, with the result that there was increased downtime and production delays; that the more expensive maintenance labor was often used to supplement direct manufacturing labor, without adequate costing or reporting, so that maintenance costs were overstated and manufacturing costs understated; and that management was not receiving adequate information about job backlogs, job cost estimates, actual job costs, and actual versus scheduled completion dates.

Zero-base budgeting itself will not uncover such detailed problems, but additional investigation into such a problem area can result in the solution required and may alter the type of zero-base budgeting and special analyses required during the planning and budgeting cycle in future years to avoid the recurrence of the problem.

The Impact of Zero-Base Budgeting

Zero-base budgeting provides management with a tremendous data base of information and analyses and can be a significant aid to operational audits in two ways:

1. Identifying problems and determining areas of potential operating and profit improvement.
2. Improving the efficiency and effectiveness of the operational audit.

Since management does not have unlimited manpower resources, it must effectively identify problems and areas of profit potential on which to concentrate its efforts, and must be able to perform the audit efficiently and effectively.

Zero-base budgeting aids managers in identifying problems and determining areas of potential operating and profit improvement by providing managers with:

- Historical cost data and performance measures for each activity.
- Comparisons of similar activities across the organization.
- Identification of duplicate activities that might be centralized.
- Identification of goals and objectives, organizational structure, and functional relationships among activities that may create or impact on a given problem.
- Alternatives (that were rejected by the operating managers who prepared the decision packages) that warrant further investigation, or obvious alternatives that were not identified or evaluated by the operating managers.

Zero-base budgeting is especially useful for centralized staffs in large organizations who can readily scan the decision packages and rankings from across the organization in their search for profitable audit areas, and can do it at a level of detail not usually available from any other source.

After management has determined the problem areas that warrant further attention, there are six steps that are usually performed in making the operational audit:

1. *Preaudit research.* Information gathering before the start of the actual audit to provide data about the area to be audited and the current state of the art, and to help determine the scope and procedures of the audit.

2. *Familiarization.* Information gathering to clearly establish the existing objectives, operating methods and procedures, operating problems, and relationships and constraints imposed by other activities or management policies.

3. *Verification.* Determining accuracy and completeness of reports, compliance of operations with existing procedures, and sampling and gathering of operating data to determine the effectiveness and efficiency of operations.

4. *Evaluation.* Determining what the operating objectives and procedures should be to produce the greatest impact on profits and operating effectiveness.

5. *Recommendation and reporting.* Summary of audit findings, specific changes recommended, and the anticipated impact of the changes.

6. *Postaudit analysis.* Follow-up to determine if the audit recommendations were implemented, produced the desired results, or require modifications or further investigation.

These basic steps will normally be followed by assigning an individual or group of individuals to evaluate and report on the problem area, with the exact nature of the effort varying with the nature of the activity audited and the background and expertise of the individuals performing the audit.

Zero-base budgeting can be a significant aid to the individuals performing the operational audit since it can impact all audit steps:

Audit Step	Impact of Zero-Base Budgeting
1. Preaudit research	Zero-base budgeting provides a ready-made reference library for managers undertaking an operational audit. The decision packages for a period of several years can be reviewed for the specific operation being audited, for similar operations in other parts of the organization, and for other activities that may influence or be influenced by the operation being audited. This research will include a more detailed evaluation of the information that led to the audit, and may indicate areas of additional research relating to specific practices, management or control techniques, and state of the art.

Audit Step	Impact of Zero-Base Budgeting
2. Familiarization	Decision packages define the objectives and interrelationships of the activities for the operation being audited, describe the nature of each activity, and identify costs and performance measures for each activity. This information provides a framework to which the auditor can add detailed information and operating procedures, and from which he can identify other meaningful performance measures not displayed on the packages.
3. Verification	Decision packages identify specific costs, benefits, and performance measures against which actual data can be compared at a functional level and detail not available in most reporting systems. The operational audit offers a separate and independent appraisal of operations and can be used to verify management reports as well as decision package information on which the budget was based.
4. Evaluation	Evaluation is a continuous process that begins when the auditor is looking for potential audit areas, so zero-base budgeting affects evaluation in the ways already mentioned (such as comparing costs and performance of similar activities). In addition, the data base provided by zero-base budgeting makes it easier for the auditor to identify operations outside his initial audit scope that are affected by any proposed changes in general policy and procedures, and to evaluate the impact that any recommended change in policy and procedures will have on all operations. Decision packages will sometimes identify excellent alternatives that were rejected by individual managers because they felt constrained by existing practices that they did not control. These

Audit Step	Impact of Zero-Base Budgeting
	practices can be challenged by the operational audit.
5. Recommendation and reporting	The decision packages and rankings provide a well-defined framework from which recommended audit changes can be explained to and evaluated by top management, changes in costs and performance can be compared, and any resulting cost and performance improvements incorporated into the budget and control systems.
6. Postaudit analysis	Zero-base budgeting offers a natural reporting and update process, with the decision packages in years subsequent to an audit reflecting changes (or lack of changes) brought about through the audit recommendations. Centralized audit staffs, or division or corporate managers, can readily keep tabs on many operations over a number of years.

Zero-base budgeting therefore allows management to perform a more effective audit by directing the auditor's attention to the most promising audit areas, and allows the auditor to be more efficient since he would be forced to develop much of the information and analysis himself that he is handed by the zero-base budgeting process.

CONCLUSION

Management is faced with the problem of coordinating a broad scope of dissimilar activities such as those illustrated in Exhibit 1-7 in Chapter 1. These activities must be balanced to ensure effective and efficient operations, which indicates the need for centralized coordination and direction. However, management is also faced with operating problems that are complicated by several factors:

1. Increasing size, diversity, and complexity of organizations.
2. Wide geographic dispersion.
3. Rapidly changing technology.

4. Increased sophistication and specialization of technology.

5. Diverse product lines or services rendered.

6. Increased need for specialized services in taxes, banking, health, environmental control, investor relations, purchasing, data processing, and so on.

These factors, as well as lengthy lists of problems specific to each organization, create the need for decentralized operations, with increased delegation of responsibility and arm's-length administration and control exercised by top management. Zero-base budgeting meets management's divergent needs for centralized coordination and direction with decentralized operations and all it includes. Zero-base budgeting is a top-down, bottom-up, top-down planning and budgeting process:

> *Top-down* because top management must determine the goals and objectives of each major organizational entity and establish the general operating guidelines and expenditure levels acceptable in achieving the objectives.
>
> *Bottom-up* because the operating managers responsible for each activity have the opportunity to evaluate their own operations and recommend a course of action to achieve the organization's objectives.
>
> *Top-down* because top management can take the recommendations and priorities established by the operating organizations, make any desired changes, and allocate the organization's resources accordingly.

Zero-base budgeting can aid management in developing a fully integrated control system that:

1. Establishes clear-cut goals and objectives.

2. Measures progress toward those goals and objectives.

3. Indicates positive action required if performance deviates from plan and budget.

4. Displays potential for further improvement.

Zero-base budgeting requires that macroeconomic goals and objectives be established for the organization, then proceeds to define the microeconomic goals and objectives for each activity. It provides both budget and performance measures as well as operating objectives, so management's control and reporting systems can indicate both budget and performance variances. These variances at the budget unit or cost center levels can be evaluated in detail by analyzing the several activities and series of decision packages from which the cost center's budget and performance capabilities were determined, and can therefore help pinpoint the specific action required that might affect only a few of the activities performed. The detailed evaluation of performance measures is especially important in the overhead, service, and support activities applicable to zero-base budgeting since budget variances for these operations are poor indicators of performance. Zero-base budgeting also aids management's operational auditing efforts by identifying problems and areas of potential operating and profit improvement as well as improving the efficiency and effectiveness of the operational audit itself.

Perhaps the greatest long range impact that zero-base budgeting will have on improving management effectiveness will result when the basic philosophy and analytic procedures become ingrained in management's thinking, or psyche. Webster's dictionary defines psyche as "the mind considered as an organic system reaching all parts of the body and serving to adjust the total organism to the needs and demands of the environment." After going through the zero-base budgeting process several times, many managers will get in the habit of evaluating alternative ways to solve a problem, considering various levels of effort, and evaluating the relative importance and priorities of problems and needs competing for attention and limited resources—not only during the formal planning and budgeting process, but during the operating year as well, as they are faced with changing situations.

The purpose of this book has been to identify the significant operating tool and impact that zero-base budgeting can provide to all levels of management in both industry and government, and to identify the flexibility and adaptations available so that each organization can adapt zero-base budgeting to its own particular needs. We hope that the discussion throughout the book leads to the conclusion that:

Zero-base budgeting is a practical management process and a part of the psyche that extends beyond the range of typical planning and budgeting techniques to impact all segments of the management domain.

SAMPLE ZERO-BASE BUDGETING MANUAL

PURPOSE OF MANUAL

The following manual is directed at those managers who will be developing decision packages. Therefore, the manual emphasizes what zero-base budgeting will do for the managers involved in the process, identifies the type of analysis each manager must make to develop his decision packages, and provides detailed instructions for completing the decision package and ranking forms. The manual does not go into detail about the organizational level at which decision packages will be developed, since this decision should be made by top level management and the "Zero-Base Budgeting Manuals" distributed to those managers designated by top management (see Chapter 3 on "Where Should Decision Packages Be Developed"). The attached manual is also very brief on the ranking process, since the managers preparing the decision packages will not have the volume or evaluation problems experienced by top management (see Chapter 5 on "Procedures for an Effective Ranking Process"). Separate sets of instructions or suggestions can be prepared for division managers responsible for organizing and coordinating zero-base budgeting since the inclusion of such extra data in all manuals has a strong tendency to confuse the lower level managers preparing packages since the information is not pertinent to them.

MANUAL CONTENTS

Any manual should contain a brief explanation of the purpose of zero-base budgeting, a thorough description of the philosophy and procedures involved (concept of decision packages, formulation of decision packages, and a brief description of the ranking process), and detailed instructions and examples for the decision package and ranking forms. When choosing an example for the manual, try to pick a straightforward and readily understandable one from an actual activity to make the discussion more meaningful and realistic. Using an example from industry for government, or vice versa, leaves most operating managers cold. However, there are hundreds of different activities within or among agencies or divisions, so one good example readily displaying the type of analysis required can be almost as effective as many examples, since we could not possibly develop an example for each potential activity.

Using one or two standard examples in a manual also allows the development of a single manual for all agencies or divisions, to which each agency or division can add any special instructions required. After the first year's implementation, new managers doing zero-base budgeting for the first time have the decision packages from the past year to use as a reference, which eliminates the problem of finding an example meaningful to each manager's activity. It is also suggested that sample forms for the additional levels of effort (i.e., package 2 of 3, package 3 of 3) be displayed in addition to the minimum level package, since developing several packages for one activity creates the greatest problem for operating managers in understanding zero-base budgeting and correctly filling out the forms.

It may also be helpful to include a letter of introduction in the manual from a top level manager in the organization, whether it is the president of a company, the governor of a state, or a top level division or agency manager. Exhibit A-1 shows the letter of introduction from Governor Jimmy Carter, which was the first page in Georgia's zero-base budgeting manual. As I mentioned previously, top level management support is vital for the successful implementation of any new process. The managers developing the decision packages usually do not have extensive contact with these top level executives, and a statement of top level support (including the statement that budgets will be determined through the zero-base budgeting process) lends necessary backing and weight to the importance of the effort.

Zero-Base Budgeting Manual

Contents

Letter of Introduction
Purpose of Zero-Base Budgeting
General Philosophy and Procedures of Zero-Base Budgeting
- Concept of Decision Packages
- Example of Production Planning
- Formulation of Decision Packages
- Decision Package Ranking

Instructions and Examples for Zero-Base Budgeting Forms
- Decision Package
- Decision Package Instructions and Definitions
- Decision Package Ranking

Attachments (Provided by Each Division)
- Calendar of Events
- Planning Assumptions and Expenditure Guidelines

Exhibit A-1 Letter of Introduction

Executive Department
Atlanta 30334

Jimmy Carter
GOVERNOR

March 15, 1971

M E M O R A N D U M

TO: All Heads of Executive Agencies and Heads of State Authorities

FROM: Governor Jimmy Carter

SUBJECT: F. Y. 1973 Budget Preparation: Zero-Base Budgeting

For the F. Y. 1973 Budget we shall adopt the concept of "Zero-Base Budgeting". This process will permit a detailed analysis and justification of Budget requests by enabling you to identify, evaluate, and rank in order of importance each function and operation which your Agency will perform.

This process will permit you and your internal management to present information and analyses needed for the Budget Director and Legislature to better understand your operations and will provide to each of you more direct control over your budgets.

Each of you will have two reviews with me to discuss your Agency's operations and your recommendations. The first review will give you the opportunity early in the Summer to present your own department's plans for the next fiscal year. The second review will give you the opportunity to update and revise your budget requests, if necessary.

Zero-Base Budgeting will assist us in re-evaluating your Agency's functions, operations, and programs and will encourage you and me to use imagination in identifying better and/or cheaper methods of operations. This process offers a challenge which I hope you will meet with enthusiasm.

PURPOSE OF ZERO-BASE BUDGETING

In most cases, plans and budgets are developed by taking the current level of operation and cost, adding "built-in" adjustments to the running rate, such as salary increases, and then requesting additional expenditures and programs. This process does not require us to review in detail the ongoing operations and expenditure levels, has led to ever increasing budgets, and *puts the burden of proof on the top management review process* to alter these budget requests.

For the 1973 budget, we are going to adopt the concept of zero-base budgeting, which requires each manager to justify his entire budget request in detail, and *shifts the burden of proof to each manager* to justify why he should spend any money. This procedure requires that all activities and operations be identified in "decision packages," which will be evaluated and ranked in order of importance by systematic analysis.

What will zero-base budgeting do for division managers?

1. The identification of 100% of each activity and operation (termed zero-base budgeting) requires each manager to evaluate and consider the need for each function and to consider different levels of effort and alternative ways for performing the function.

2. Each activity or cost center manager will have the opportunity to evaluate his operations in depth, to evaluate alternatives, and to communicate his analysis and recommendations to higher management for their review and consideration in determining budget allocations.

3. Once decision packages have been identified and given a priority ranking, changes in desired expenditure levels for division budgets do not require the recycling of budget inputs, but the decision package ranking identifies those activities or operations (decision packages) to be added or deleted.

4. The list of ranked decision packages can be used during the operating year to identify activities to be reduced or expanded if allowable expenditure levels change or actual costs vary from the budget.

The philosophy, procedures, and budget forms and instructions for zero-base budgeting are described in this manual. The instructions have been kept short and allow a great deal of flexibility in adapting the general concepts and procedures to your specific needs. This process has only two forms, which are intended to aid each manager in planning and budgeting his activities (not a form to be filled out after the planning and budgeting process is completed).

GENERAL PHILOSOPHY AND PROCEDURES OF ZERO-BASE BUDGETING

Concept of Decision Packages

A decision package identifies a discrete function or operation in a definitive manner for management evaluation and comparison with other functions, including consequences of not performing that function, alternative courses of action, and costs and benefits. Decision packages will be defined at functional or operating levels at or below the cost center level in most divisions, where discrete pieces of an operation can have meaningful identification and evaluation.

There are two types of alternatives that should be considered when developing decision packages:

1. *Different ways of performing the same function.* This analysis identifies alternative ways of performing a function. The best alternative is chosen and the others are discarded:

- If an alternative to the current way of doing business is chosen, the recommended way should be shown in the decision package with the current way shown as an alternative.
- Only one decision package is prepared. It shows the recommended way of performing the function and identifies the alternative ways considered, giving a brief explanation of why they were not chosen.

2. *Different levels of effort of performing the function.* This analysis identifies alternative levels of effort to perform a specific or related function. A minimum level of effort should be established, and additional levels of effort identified as separate decision packages:

- This minimum level of effort package may not completely achieve the purpose of the function (even the additional levels of effort proposed may not completely achieve it because of realistic budget and achievement levels), but it should identify and attack the most important elements. In many cases the minimum level of effort will be from 50 to 70% of the current level of operation. (One exception to this rule of thumb would be start-up functions or operations that were not up to full speed during the preceding budget year).
- The minimum level of effort package would be ranked higher than the additional level(s) of effort so that the elimination of these lower

ranked packages does not preclude the performance of higher ranked packages.

Managers should consider both types of alternatives in identifying and evaluating each function. Managers will usually identify different ways of performing the same function first, and then evaluate different levels of effort for performing the function for whatever way or method chosen.

Example of Production Planning

The following example of production planning illustrates the type of analysis that each manager needs to make to prepare his decision packages.

The production planning manager analyzed his department's purpose and efforts and decided that decision packages should be developed around production planning as a whole rather than around each separate work unit (such as working with marketing to determine delivery schedules, estimating production time and material needs, or preparing schedules) since he had a small department and each work unit took only a fraction of the daily effort. He then proceeded to make the following analysis:

1. *Different ways of performing the same function.*
   (a) *Recommended decision package.* Production planning department for product X, with five production planners (cost— $60,000). Maintain current organization and method of operation. This level of effort is required to maintain shipping and production schedules and inventory reports updated at the level desired by the manufacturing superintendent..
   (b) *Alternatives not recommended.*
      • Eliminate production planners and let line foremen do their own planning (zero incremental cost for foremen). This would result in excessive inventories, inefficient production runs, and delayed shipments.
      • Combine production planning for products X, Y, and Z. This would save two planners at $15,000 each (total of 12 planners for combined departments), but foremen of each product line fear lack of specialized service; peak work loads on all product lines coincide, creating excessive burden for one supervisor;

product departments are in separate buildings and physical proximity of planning is desired.

The analysis of functions and operations should not stop at this point, but each manager should consider different levels of effort for performing the function. Different levels of effort should be considered and identified when they are realistic alternatives for two reasons:

1. The functional level managers who develop these decision packages are better equipped (because of their detailed knowledge of that particular function) to identify and evaluate different levels of effort, and it should be the responsibility of these managers to advise higher management of these possibilities. It then becomes higher management's responsibility to evaluate the relative importance of functions and different levels of effort within each function.

2. Limited expenditure levels (due to dollar constraints and the desired funding of new or expanding programs) would cause the complete elimination of some functions if only one decision package at some desired level of effort were identified. Such elimination *might not* be desirable and practical and higher management might prefer to have the option of reducing levels of effort rather than eliminating entire functions.

Continuing with our same example for production planning, different levels of effort might be identified as follows:

Product X planning (1 of 3): cost—$45,000
> Four planners required for minimum planning support and coordination between marketing and manufacturing, and for establishing production schedules and making reports. Would reduce longer range planning, inventory control, and marketing support for special product modifications.

Product X planning (2 of 3): cost—$15,000
> One long range planner required to increase forward planning of production and shipping schedules from 2 to 4 weeks, to update in-process inventory reports daily rather than every other day (to aid inventory control), and to assist marketing manager with customers who require special product modifications. (Current level of staffing.)

Product X planning (3 of 3): cost—$15,000
> One operations research analyst required to evaluate optimal

length of production run versus optimal inventory levels by color and size or product. (Savings of 1% in production cost or a reduction of 5% in inventory level would offset this added cost.)

For most functions, different levels of effort should be possible. By developing these different levels as separate decision packages the functional manager is stating that he thinks all levels deserve serious consideration within realistic funding expectations, but he is identifying these possible levels and leaving it to higher management to make trade-offs among functions and level of effort within each function.

However, if different levels of effort are not realistic because of the specific circumstances involved, only one decision package at the recommended level of effort should be identified, with the reasons given for choosing that level. For the preceding example, the level of production planning effort might have been specified by the manufacturing manager for product X, who thought that any cost reductions or changes from the specified effort were of minor consideration compared to the resulting production problems or increased manufacturing costs and risks.

The identification and analysis of alternatives and the following preparation of decision packages cannot be made in a vacuum. Guidelines concerning direction and purpose should be provided by organizational managers to coordinate the development of packages, and preparatory discussions with those affected by the packages should be held. In the preceding example, the preparation of production planning decision packages should have been made only after discussions with the production and marketing managers whose work is affected by the type and amount of production planning.

Formulation of Decision Packages

Decision packages are usually formulated at or below the cost center level to promote a detailed identification of functions, operations, and alternatives by those managers most familiar with the task to be performed, and to generate interest in and commitment by those individuals who will be responsible for carrying out the actions identified in the approved packages. To begin developing decision packages, a manager might logically start by identifying the current year's operations. The manager can take the current year's expenditure level, identify the functions or operations creating this expense, and calculate or estimate the cost for each function. After current operations have been

Chart A. Procedure for Formulating Decision Packages

All Decision Packages Ranked Together

Different ways and/or levels of effort to perform the function identified and evaluated

Functions where there are no logical alternatives, or the present method or level of operation is chosen

Decision Packages Developed for new functions or operations

Assumptions: Expenditure guidelines, Activity levels, people to be served, wage + salary increases, etc.

"Business as Usual" levels of effort identified for the upcoming budget year

Current Operating levels Broken into Discrete Functions or Operations

Business as Usual:

FY 1972 costs, for 1972 functions projected into 1973, with no change in the method of operations. This cost is obtained by taking 1972 expense, and adjusting for: (a) salary increases, (b) annualizing employees who were not on the payroll for a full year, but will be employed at year end 1972, and (c) changes in the level of effort or requirements for dependent service functions

"Preparation of Decision Packages"

"Orientation and Background Analysis"

Cost Centers or Activities within a Division

broken into decision packages, the managers can start looking at the requirements for the coming year.

The procedure for formulating decision packages is shown on Chart A. The identification of "business as usual" levels of effort merely provides the basis from which each manager will consider next year's operating requirements. The real starting point in determining next year's budget occurs when alternatives to "business as usual" levels of effort are developed by evaluating different ways and/or levels of effort to perform the function. If an alternative to the "business as usual" method is chosen, the so-called alternative method is incorporated into the recommended package and the "business as usual" method is identified as the alternative. At the conclusion of the formulation stage the manager will have identified the proposed functions, which will fall into three categories:

1. Different ways and/or different levels of effort for performing the function.

2. "Business as usual," where there are no logical alternatives or the present method and level of effort is recommended.

3. Packages for new functions or operations.

The manager is now ready to rank these packages.

Decision Package Ranking

This section suggests some ranking procedures that may be of help to each manager in ranking his decision packages. The ranking process attempts to provide management with a technique to allocate its limited resources by answering:

1. What goals should we attempt to achieve?
2. How much should we spend in this attempt?

Management can try to answer these questions by taking the decision packages identified and listing (ranking) them in order of decreasing benefit to each organization. Management could then identify both the benefits to be gained at each expenditure level and the consequences of not approving additional packages ranked below that expenditure level.

The initial ranking of packages should occur at the organizational level where the packages are developed in order to allow each manager to evaluate the relative importance of his own function or operations.

This ranking will be reviewed at higher organizational levels and used as a guide for merging those rankings. At the lower organizational levels, rankings can be done by an individual if he has detailed knowledge of the areas involved. However, at the higher levels the expertise required to rank packages may be best obtained by use of a committee.

Two problem areas can be expected during the initial implementation of the ranking process:

1. Managers may have conceptual difficulty in ranking packages that they consider "requirements" and may express concern as to their ability to judge the relative importance of dissimilar functions since many packages require subjective judgment.

2. The number of decision packages may be too great for the time management has available to thoroughly evaluate and rank the packages.

The difficulty and the time consumed in ranking packages can be reduced if managers:

1. Do not concentrate on ranking packages that are high priority or "requirements" and are well within the expenditure guidelines (other than to ensure that all alternatives, cost reduction opportunities, and operating improvements have been explored and incorporated as appropriate) but instead concentrate on discretionary functions and levels of effort.

2. Do not spend too much time worrying whether package 4 is more important than package 5, but only assure themselves that packages 4 *and* 5 are more important than package 15, and package 15 more important than package 25, and so on.

Ranking packages at each organizational level allows the responsible managers to evaluate the desirability of various expenditure levels throughout the planning and budgeting process. Teams consisting of budget department and division managers will be assigned to assist managers in preparing and ranking packages, and should be contacted with any questions relating to zero-base budgeting.

INSTRUCTIONS AND EXAMPLES FOR ZERO-BASE BUDGETING FORMS

Before the forms can be meaningful, you must read the preceding section concerning the "General Philosophies and Procedures of Zero-Base Budgeting."

Decision Package

This form (2 pages) may serve as the entire presentation for a decision package, or it may serve as a summary sheet for a package (each section should be complete in itself, with no sentences continuing onto additional pages). There may be as many attached descriptive, backup, and analysis sheets as desired.

Purpose. To identify the 1973 proposed activities, functions, operations, alternatives, and related costs in a definitive manner for management evaluation and comparison to other activities, functions, or operations.

Prepared By. All managers of discrete functions, activities, or operations (usually at or below the cost center level).

Submitted To. As specified by higher levels of management, including immediate organizational superior and Division Controller.
(*Note:* All forms should be typed.)

Decision Package Instructions and Definitions

1. *Package name.* Descriptive title of function or operation that is the subject of the package. If there are several levels of effort being recommended for the function or operation, the package name should be shown as follows:
   • Title (1 of *n*)
   • Title (2 of *n*)
   to identify the level of effort the package represents.
2. *Division.* Name of division (abbreviation is acceptable).
3. *Department.* Product department, profit center, or major organizational unit within the division.
4. *Cost center.* Cost center number (cost center name may also be included).
5. *Ranking.* Initial ranking of manager responsible for preparation of decision packages, in order of descending importance of priority (i.e., package ranked number 1 is more important than package number 2). At subsequent review levels these packages may be renumbered when these rankings are merged with those of other organizational units.
6. *Statement of purpose.* Describe the purpose of this decision package

in relation to a problem this package is attempting to solve or a service this package is attempting to provide (goals, objectives).

7. *Description of actions (operations).* State and describe the methods, actions, or operations necessary to perform the package (i.e., what will you do and how will you do it?).

8. *Achievements/benefits.* Identify the tangible results to be realized through performance of the package, with emphasis on quantitative results (quantitative measures may be shown on section 10 of the form). Achievements should identify how the package partially or completely achieves the purpose (as stated in section 6) or solves the problem, and should highlight any improvement in efficiency or effectiveness.

9. *Consequences of not approving package.* In addition to not obtaining the achievements identified in section 8, what impact will this have on other functions, activities, or operations? Identify any policy or procedure changes that would have to be made if the package were not approved.

10. *Quantitative package measures.* Give meaningful quantitative measures to assist managers in evaluating the package and the effectiveness of performance. Include cost effectiveness, ratios, unit cost, problem trends, work load measures (i.e., number of units of work performed) that the package is designed to achieve or effect.

11. *Resources required (dollars in thousands).*
    - Gross expense: Total cost incurred for that activity including charges from other activities within the same organization. (*Charge-outs:* costs charged to user activities for direct services provided by this activity.)
    - Net expense: Gross expense minus charge-outs.
    - People: The number of hourly and salaried employees required.
    - 1971/1972 expense and people: 1971 actual expense, and people on board at year-end; 1972 projected expense and people on board at year-end.
    - % 73/72: The percent of 1973 expense and people as compared to 1972 expense and people, derived by dividing 1973 amounts by 1972 amounts.

Note: If the package being prepared has different levels of effort, the 1971 and 1972 information is shown on the minimum level package (package 1 of n) with subsequent level packages showing only the 1973 costs associated with that package. However, the % 73/72 . . . for packages above the minimum level should show the cumulative level of 1973 expense versus 1972 expense.

	1972	1973	73/72	Calculations
Package (1 of 3)	60	45	75%	(45) ÷ 60 = 75%
Package (2 of 3)		15	100%	(45 + 15) ÷ 60 = 100%
Package (3 of 3)		15	125%	(45 + 15 + 15) ÷ 60 = 125%

(The same is true for people numbers.)

12. *Alternatives (different levels of effort) and cost.*
   (a) Decision packages for a function or operation identifying different levels of effort. The package name, cost, and a brief description of the package(s) for the other levels of effort for that function or operation should be shown (separate packages will be prepared for these other levels of effort).
   • For example, package (1 of 3) would display the summary information for packages (2 of 3) and (3 of 3); package (2 of 3) would display the summary for packages (1 of 3) and (3 of 3), and package (3 of 3) would display the summary of packages (1 of 3) and (2 of 3).
   • This display information is provided so that an individual looking at only one package could see the total levels of effort being recommended for that function or operation.
   (b) Decision packages for a function or operation *not* identifying different levels of effort. Give a brief explanation of why a lower level of effort was not possible and/or recommended.
13. *Alternatives (different ways of performing the function, activity, or operation).* Realistic alternatives to the recommended means of performing the function should be described, the reason for rejection stated, and the cost of the alternatives estimated if possible. Realistic alternatives to the chosen alternative should be displayed on each decision package, whether that package is the minimum level of effort or represents an additional level of effort.
14. *Detail costing.* The spaces provided for detail costing should aid each manager in estimating his costs, with the gross and net costs equaling the costs shown in section 11 on the first page of the decision package form.
   • Additional accounts may be added in the blank spaces provided.
   • Costs may be estimated in thousands, hundreds, or whole dollars. A decimal point should be used if costs are estimated below whole thousands of dollars. Totals for gross and net do not have to total an even thousand dollars, with a rounding to the nearest thousand dollars shown in section 11.

Decision Package

(1) Package Name	(2) Division	(3) Department	(4) Cost Center	(5) Rank
Product X Planning (1 of 3)	Circuits	DTL Planning	205	2

(6) Statement of Purpose

Provide minimum level of planning effort for Product X, with an estimated 5.8 million production units, to provide production and shipping schedules for the line foreman.

(7) Description of Actions (Operations)

Maintain updated production and shipping schedules for two weeks in advance (currently maintaining schedules four weeks in advance).

Provide finished goods inventory level reports daily and in process inventory reports every other day (currently being done daily).

Maintain perpetual inventory system (computerized) on raw materials to maintain a two week supply on hand and a two week supply on order.

Two accounting clerks, two planners.

(8) Achievements/Benefits

Activity required for minimum maintenance of planning function to deliver products on schedule. Overtime and clerical effort reduced due to perpetual inventory system. Professional replaced with clerk for a savings of $6,000.

(9) Consequences of not Approving Package

Elimination of planners would force line foremen to do their own planning (zero incremental cost for foremen); but excessive inventories, inefficient production runs, and delayed shipments would result in excessive sales loss.

(10) Quantitative Package

Measures	1971	1972	1973
$ million NSB/planner	3.75	3.60	5.25
Average inventory/$ million NSB	10%	12%	12%
Package cost/NSB	.30%	.33%	.21%
Package cost/GPM	.90%	1.1%	.75%

(11) Resources Required ($ in Thousands)

	1971	1972	1973	% 73/72
GROSS $	45	60	45	75%
NET $	45	60	45	75%
PEOPLE: HOURLY	1	1	2	200%
SALARY	3	4	2	50%

Manager John Adams   Prepared By John Adams   Date 7/10/72

Decision Package

(1) Package Name	(2) Division	(3) Department	(4) Cost Center	(5) Rank	
Product X Planning (1 of 3)	Circuits	DTL Planning	205	2	

(12) Alternatives (Different Levels of Effort) and Cost

- Package 2 of 3 (cost $15K): Add back long range planner. Increase forward planning of production and shipping schedules from two to four weeks, update in process inventory reports daily, assist marketing manager with special problem customers.

- Package 3 of 3 (cost $15K): Add operations research analyst to evaluate optimal length of production runs versus optimal inventory level by color and size of product.

(14) DETAIL COSTING

#	ACCOUNT	1972	1973
	WAGES	5.5	10.2
	SALARIES	38.8	21.0
	BENEFITS	5.1	3.2
211	MAINTENANCE		
215	MATL./SUPPLIES	2.3	2.0
217	DEPRECIATION	.7	.5
401	TRAVEL		
415	FEES		

(13) **Alternatives (Different Ways of Performing the Same Function, Activity, or Operation)**

1. Combine production planning for products X, Y, and Z: Save two planners at $15,000 each (total of 12 planners for combined departments). Foremen of each product line fear lack of specialized service; peak workloads on all product lines coincide—creating an excessive burden on one supervisor to effectively manage; product departments are located in separate buildings and physical proximity of planning is desired.

2. Production planning performed by line foremen: (see consequences of not approving this package).

501 TELEPHONE		1.2	1.0
502 RENT/OCCUPANCY		2.5	2.5
503 UTILITIES	.5		.5
710 Computer	3.0		3.0
ALL OTHER	.5		.5
GROSS $		60.1	45.0
NET $		60.1	45.0

(15) QUARTERLY DISTRIBUTION

	1	2	3	4
GROSS	10	11	12	12
NET	10	11	12	12
HRLY	1	2	2	2
SAL	2	2	2	2

Decision Package

(1) Package Name Product X Planning (2 of 3)	(2) Division Circuits	(3) Department DTL Planning	(4) Cost Center 205	(5) Rank 6

(6) Statement of Purpose

Provide long range planning and scheduling for product X with an estimated 5.8 million production units which fluctuates significantly by quarter (1.5 million 1st quarter, 1.8 million second quarter, 1.3 million 3rd quarter, 1.2 million 4th quarter).

(7) Description of Actions (Operations)

Increase forward planning of production and shipping schedules from two to four weeks.

Update in-process inventory reports daily rather than every other day to aid inventory control; special inventory projects; assist in monthly inventory.

Assist marketing manager with customers who require special product modifications; assist shipping department in long term projections and distribution planning.

One planner.

(8) Achievements/Benefits

Average inventory levels reduced 1 to 2%; helps avoid out of stock conditions which require special production runs; serves as liaison between marketing and production, and production and shipping.

(9) Consequences of not Approving Package

Excess inventory and operating problems; detail long range production planning eliminated because it cannot be done by line foremen or marketing managers; manufacturing supervisors must provide their own liaison with marketing and shipping.

(10) Quantitative Package Measures

Measures	1971	1972	1973
$ million NSB/Planner	3.75	3.60	4.20
Average inventory/$ million NSB	10%	12%	11%
Planning cost (1 + 2)/NSB	.30%	.33%	.29%
Planning cost (1 + 2)/GPM	.90%	1.1%	1.0%

(11) Resources Required ($ in Thousands)

	1971	1972	1973	% 73/72
GROSS $			15	100%
NET $			15	100%
PEOPLE: HOURLY				200%
SALARY			1	75%

Prepared By John Adams   Date 7/10/72

Manager John Adams

Decision Package

(1) Package Name	(2) Division	(3) Department	(4) Cost Center	(5) Rank
Product X Planning (2 of 3)	Circuits	DTL Planning	205	6

(12) Alternatives (Different Levels of Effort) and Cost

- Package 1 of 3 (cost $45K): Four planners to provide minimum planning effort to produce production and shipping schedules. Reduced long range planning, inventory control, and special marketing support.

- Package 3 of 3 (cost $15K): Add operations research analyst to evaluate optimal length of production runs versus optimal inventory level by color and size of product.

(14) DETAIL COSTING

#	ACCOUNT	1972	1973
	WAGES		
	SALARIES		12.0
	BENEFITS		1.5
211	MAINTENANCE		
215	MATL./SUPPLIES		.5
217	DEPRECIATION		
401	TRAVEL		
415	FEES		

(13) Alternatives (Different Ways of Performing the Same Function, Activity, or Operation)

1. Combine production planning for products X, Y, and Z. Foremen fear lack of specialized service, peak workloads on all product lines coincide, product departments are located in separate buildings and physical proximity of planning is desired.

2. Long range planning done by line foremen: would result in excessive inventories, inefficient production runs, and delayed shipments. Foremen would have a tough time scheduling two weeks in advance, and would probably have no time to devote to longer range planning.

3. Combine all long range production planning to the Division Marketing Department: Workloads are more directly related to production than marketing.

501	TELEPHONE	.3
502	RENT/OCCUPANCY	
503	UTILITIES	.1
710	Computer	.5
	ALL OTHER	.1
	GROSS $	15.0
	NET $	15.0

(15) QUARTERLY DISTRIBUTION	1	2	3	4
GROSS	3	4	4	4
NET	3	4	4	4
HRLY				
SAL	1	1	1	1

Decision Package Ranking

RANK	Package Name	1972 Resources			1973 Resources			Cumulative Level		
		Gross $	Net $	People HRL/SAL	Gross $	Net $	People HRL/SAL	Gross $	Net $	%*
1	Quality Control (1 of 3)	175	175	11/3	90	90	6/1	90	90	
* 2	Product X Planning (1 of 3)	60	60	1/4	45	45	2/2	135	135	
3	Routine and preventive maintenance (1 of 2)	150	150	10/2	105	105	7/1	240	240	
4	Industrial Engineering (1 of 4)	90	90	2/6	41	41	1/2	281	281	
5	Administration	23	23	1/1	25	25	1/1	306	306	
* 6	Product X Planning (2 of 3)				15	15	1	321	321	
7	Relocate test and assembly				45	45		366	366	
8	Industrial engineering (2 of 4)				35	35	3	401	401	71%
9	Routine and preventive maintenance (2 of 2)				50	50	3/1	451	451	80%
10	Maintenance scheduler	9	9	1	10	10	1	461	461	82%
11	Quality control (2 of 3)				83	83	5/1	544	544	97%
12	Industrial engineering (3 of 4)				20	20	1/1	564	564	100%

#	Cost Center or Organization Ranked									
13	Quality control (3 of 3)				30	30	2/1	594	594	105%
14 *	Product X planning (3 of 3)				15	15	1	609	609	108%
15	Records and file clerk	6	6	1	6	6	1	615	615	109%
16	Industrial Engineering (4 of 4)				15	15	1	630	630	112%
17	Computerized scheduling model				10	10		640	640	114%
	Non recurring 1972 expense	50	50							
	1972 Expense	563	563							

Sample Calculation:

$$\frac{640}{563} = 114\%$$

Cost Center or Organization Ranked	Manager	Prepared By	Date
Manufacturing Support: Product X	Bill Williams	Joe Schmidt	7/25/72

Page 1 of 1

* 1973 Cumulative *NET* $ as a % of Total FY 1972 Budgeted *NET* $ for corresponding organizations.

- If the package has several levels of effort, the detail cost estimates for 1972 should be shown on the minimum level package, with subsequent level packages showing only 1973 costs associated with that package.

15. *Quarterly distribution.* Allocate the gross and net costs (in whole thousands of dollars) quarterly. This distribution should tie to the figures shown in sections 11 and 14. People numbers should reflect people on board at the end of each quarter.

16. *Attachments.* Special analyses or additional explanations may be attached to each package at the discretion of the manager preparing the package if he thinks this additional information is required for effective evaluation of the package by higher management. Top management may also identify special analyses or information for specific cost centers. However, such attachments should be kept as brief as possible.

Decision Package Ranking

Purpose. To identify and display decision packages in order of importance and benefit to aid in the evaluation and determination of 1973 budget levels for various organizational units.

Prepared By. All managers preparing decision packages or performing ranking of decision packages. All organizations for which rankings are merged.

Submitted To. As requested by higher levels of management, including immediate organizational superior and Division Controller.

Instructions and Definitions

1. *Rank.* Rank each package in order of descending importance (i.e., package number 1 is more important than package number 2).

2. *Package name.* Name shown on the corresponding decision package form.

3. *1972 and 1973 resources.* Gross dollars, net dollars, and people (hourly and salary) as shown on the decision package.

4. *Cumulative level.* The sums of the 1973 gross and net cost for each decision package plus all packages ranked above it. Percent: 1973 cumulative net dollars divided by 1972 net dollars for the corresponding organization being ranked.

DECISION PACKAGE TOPICS

This appendix provides a sample listing of topics or activities around which decision packages have been developed in industry and government. This listing is provided to aid the reader in determining where such packages might be developed in his own organization. The topic listings have been grouped into the three broad categories of administration, technical, and commercial as illustrated in Exhibit 1-7 in Chapter 1, with some additional listings taken from various organizations in state government. These topic groupings are "laundry listings," which may not be complete for any given organization, may overlap in some cases, may be too broad in scope so that a topic should be further subdivided, or may be too narrow in scope so that several topics should be combined (see Chapter 3 on "Where Should Decision Packages be Developed?"). The following listings were taken primarily from decision packages developed by Texas Instruments, the Dillingham Corporation of Honolulu, Hawaii, and the states of Georgia and New Mexico.

ADMINISTRATION

Accounting / Control

Accounting	Timekeeping
Accounts receivable	General ledger
Accounts payable	Records
Consolidation accounting	Manufacturing overhead control
Audit—outside fees	Balance sheet reporting
Year-end audits	Forecasting and reporting
Internal audits	Accounting and information
Acquisition analysis	systems

Credit
Controller's office
Bank reconciliations
Annual planning (budgeting)
Payroll

Financial analysis
Special projects
Subsidiary control and audit
Equipment records and control

Legal

Patent acquisitions
Adversary patents
Contract negotiations
Interferences
Trade secrets
Trademarks
Patent licensing
Corporate legal compliance
Division legal support
Legal—domestic

Legal—international
Patent interferences
Litigation—defensive
Litigation—offensive
Consulting fees
Patent prosecution
Investigations
Customs cases/recovery
Contract reviews

Treasury

Treasury—international
Treasury—domestic
Cash management
Investor relations
Cashier
Bank relations
Trust services

Portfolio management
Investor records
Stockholders meetings
SEC reporting
Financial communications
Actuarial fees

Tax

Tax planning
File and defend tax returns
Property tax control
International taxes
Domestic taxes
Compliance

Federal tax compliance
State tax compliance
Ad valorem tax compliance
Tax payments (by type)
Special studies
Investment tax credit

Insurance

Risk management
Claims
Loss prevention

Product liability
Insurance management
Premiums (by type)

Personnel

Public relations
Staffing
Staffing—hourly
Staffing—salary
Compensation
Benefits
Personnel administrators
Community relations
Public affairs—contributions
     and donations
News and editorial service
College recruiting
Labor relations

Awards banquets
Training
Training programs (by program)
Job evaluation
Personnel information systems
Job description
Employee newspapers and
     personnel communications
Equal opportunity employment
Employee handbooks
Summer development program
Recreation

Data Processing

Planning
Statistical services
Technical library
Maintenance of existing programs
Modifications and improvements
     of existing programs
Systems design
Systems development
Major systems design and develop-
     ment (by project)
Programming—business/scientific

Equipment maintenance
Scheduling and control
Tape library
Equipment costs/rental
Computer aided graphics
Time sharing
Standard procedures administration
Systems audits
Computer operations
Terminal operations
Keypunch

General Overhead and Support

Supervision (all departments)
Administration (all departments)
Secretarial pools
Cleaning/janitorial
Special cleaning
Automotive services
Trash hauling
Cafeteria/food
Telephone
Telephone—operators/switchboard
Telephone—equipment
Telephone—long distance and
    WATTS lines
Safety and security
Fire department
Health services
Travel and reservations
Traffic police

Guard posts
Physical security
Military security
Mail
Postage
Site access control
Receptionist and visitor control
President's office
Board of Directors
Corporation and division officers
Printing
Photography
Retirement, group insurance, and
    other benefits not allocated
Credit union
Special costs
Landscaping and grounds
    maintenance

TECHNICAL

Research and Development

Major projects (by project)
Minor projects (by type, category,
    specialities required, etc.)
Laboratory testing (by lab, type
    of testing, etc.)
Applied research

Equipment
Technical support
Administrative support
Libraries
Pure research

Maintenance

Routine maintenance
Preventive maintenance
Production assistance
Major projects (by project)
Major repairs (by project)

Spare parts
Spare parts control
Building maintenance
Effluents control
Moves and rearrangements

Production Planning and Control

Production planning
Customer interface
Inventory control
Material control and forecasting
Billings forecasting
Market projections and
    interpretation

Line balancing
Demand balancing
Work scheduling
Long range planning
Equipment planning
Systems development

Quality Control

Quality control (by factory,
    product line, product)
Destructive testing

In-process goods testing
Finished goods testing
Raw material testing

Industrial Engineering

Industrial engineering (by division,
    plant, department, product
    line, product)
Special projects
Work measurement
Job evaluation
Safety
Standardization/manuals

Plant design and layout
Equipment procurement and
    replacement
Operations analysis
Materials handling
Methods engineering
Tool design
Process design

Facilities Planning and Development

Facilities planning
Architectural
Drafting
Facilities development
Construction supervision
Site selection

Property management
Space accounting and reporting
Lease management
Facilities installation
Construction teams

Other Technical

Product design
Drafting
Manufacturing engineering

Technicians (by type)
Engineering (by type)

COMMERCIAL

Sales

Advertising
Corporate image advertising
Product advertising
Promotion
Regional marketing administration
Sales force
Order processing
Customer credit
Test marketing

Market research
Mail order
Catalogs
Brochures
Giveaways
Automated ordering systems
Sales forecasting
Sales planning and development
Dealerships/middlemen

Purchasing and Supply

Purchasing (total, by organization,
    type of material purchased)
Contracts for bid
Contract negotiation
Invoice processing and approval
Purchase order processing
Automated ordering systems

Stockroom
Property control/inventory
Surplus property control
Inventory control
Clerical/records
Invoice posting/auditing

Transportation and Distribution

Transportation (by product or
    product line)
Distribution (by product or
    product line)
Shipping
Receiving
Scheduling

Warehousing/storage
Marketing and production liaison
Automated inventory/location
    systems
Carrier negotiations
Inventory control

HOSPITAL (MENTAL)

Administration (see other listing)
Admissions
Medical records
Doctors (by speciality)
Nurses (by speciality)
Attendants
Dentistry
Psychology
Psychiatry
Radiology
Pathology
Laboratory (by lab)
Morgue
Occupational therapy
Recreational therapy
Music therapy
Research (see separate listing)
Sociological research
Experimental psychopathology
Behavioral assessment
Special clinics
Medical library
Food service
Police/security
Ambulance
Surgery
Rehabilitation (by program)

Social work
Property control
Laundry
Commissary
Maintenance
Housekeeping
Engineering and plant operations
Outpatient service
Disposal and sewage
Chaplain
Volunteer services
Special patient services
Community relations
Purchasing
Training (by program)
Pharmacy
Psychiatric training
Genetics
Family research
Neurology
Audiovisual services
Facility improvements/additions
    (by project)
Equipment (groupings for minor
    items, by item for major
    expenditures)

PUBLIC SAFETY (POLICE)

Highway patrol (total, by post,
    breakouts within each post—
    see example in Chapter 3)
Field supervision
Records and identification
Dispatching
Pathology
Criminalistics laboratory
Drug identification

Revocation and suspension
    (drivers' license)
Civil disorder unit
Firearms control
Accident report processing
Training
License pickup
Vehicles—purchasing,
    maintenance, supply

Toxicology laboratory
Handwriting analysis
Branch crime laboratories
Implied consent
Intelligence squad
Narcotics squad
Polygraph operations
Headquarters security
Commercial driver training school
Motor vehicle inspection
Drivers' license issuance

Uninsured motorists
Point system (violations)
Microfilm inactive drivers'
  licenses
Auto theft squad
Police academy
Equipment/facilities (groupings,
  individual items)
Administration (see separate
  listing)

WELFARE (STATE LEVEL)

Grant Programs (to local agencies)

AFDC
Aged
Blind
Disabled
Family foster care
Institutional foster care
Work incentive
Maternity

Day care
Emergency assistance
Specialized foster care
Return of runaway children
Psychological, psychiatric, and
  speech therapy
Emergency shelter homes

State-Supplied Services

Eligibility determination
County administration
Food programs
Child welfare services
Interviewing and correspondence
Quality control (aid programs)
Medical eligibility
Consultant physicians
Policy development and
  dissemination
Youth services
Court services
Treatment of delinquents

Social workers/caseworkers (by
  program, location)
Research
Federal project services
Benefits control unit
Educational leave and scholarships
Library
Statistical unit
Hearing officers
Public relations
Adoption services
Physical examinations
Work training

Court service workers
Court field representatives

Licensing
Vocational guidance

Institutions

Institution (separate, groupings of smaller units)

Activity breakouts within each institution (see hospital example)

AGRICULTURE

Inspection and testing (field operations, by type—feed, fertilizer, pesticides, seed, meat, poultry, blood, hatchery, etc.)
Weights and measures
Air sampling of hatcheries
Entomology
Foundation seed operation
Animal disease eradication
Animal disease diagnosis
Quality milk program
Bonding and certification
Commodity promotion
Press and radio
News service

Laboratory testing (by lab, by type —poultry, animal disease, pathology, brucellosis)
Farmers' markets
Grain grading
Livestock market news
Consumers' market bulletin
Consumer protection
Equine program
Beekeeping
Field inspections
Advertising
Fire ant eradication
Crop reporting service
Seed technology
Egg quality control

HIGHWAY

Construction

Authority lease rentals
Bond payments

Capital projects (groupings, by project)

Planning and Construction Support

Bridge design
Bridge construction liaison

Branch laboratories
Aggregate testing

Bridge inventory
Road design
Location studies
Photogrammetry
Road and traffic statistics
Planning
Planning studies
Research and development
Asphalt design
Soil investigation
Soil testing

Pit section
Materials audit
Surveys
Right of way
Traffic engineering
Field engineering
Residences
Construction supervision
Capital projects and equipment
Permit review

Maintenance and Betterments

Routine maintenance
Maintenance shop
Concrete paving repair
Bridge maintenance
Asphalt crews
Sign department
Grassing crews

Grading crews
Carpenter crews
Heavy maintenance
Radio and communications
Traffic markings
Painting
Capital projects and equipment

UNIVERSITY

Instruction

Departments (by department)
Courses (by course, groupings)
Department administration
Instructional support (computer, other services)

Laboratories
New courses (by course)
"Chairs"
Formula (based on student enrollment, credit hours, student/ teacher ratios)

Research

Research (see separate listing)
Grants

Research fellowships

Libraries

Librarians
Book binding
Cataloging
Photocopy and microfilm
Research
Special projects
Renovations

New book purchases
Subscriptions
General service—checkout, reader
    assistance
Computer
Filing
Capital projects/equipment

Administrative

(See separate listing)
Office of the President
Office of the Provost
Admissions
Graduate admissions
Registrar
Evaluation and remedial counseling
University relations
Health services
Housing
Student judicial affairs
Testing and evaluation

Alumni relations
Trust funds
Police department
Fire department
Student activities/union
Career development
Student employment/placement
Financial aid services
Placement and student aid
Student loans
Information and publications
Computer services

GAME AND FISH DEPARTMENT

Administration (see separate
    listing)
Area offices
District offices
Aircraft
Radio communications
Warehouse
Licensing
Law enforcement
Coastal patrol
Wildlife resource management

Fish research
Fish hatcheries
Coastal fisheries—resource
    management
Coastal fisheries—research and
    development
Fish protection
Management of private and public
    waters
Capital outlay (groupings, by
    project)

Hunter training
Wildlife investigations
Wildlife stocking and control
Federal aid development
Land acquisition
Game research

Public relations
Vehicle fleet operations
Vehicle maintenance
Out-of-state promotion
Wildlife magazine
Fishing magazine

INDEX